When Your Heels Need To Be Healed

A Journey to Freedom and Wholeness

APOSTLE FREE HILL

Published by Gospel 4 U Publishing

412 E. North Street

Carlisle PA 17013

1-844-4U-GOSPEL

www.gospel4unetwork.com

ISBN-13 (Paperback): 978-0692416990

Library of Congress Control Number: 2015937318

Unless otherwise noted, Scripture quotations are from The Amplified Bible, © 1965 Zondervan Publishing House. Used by permission.

Definitions are from *dictionary.com* and *Collins English Dictionary - Complete & Unabridged* 10th Edition 2009 © William Collins Sons & Co. Ltd. 1979, 1986 © HarperCollins Publishers 1998, 2000, 2003, 2005, 2006, 2007, 2009, 2012

Printed in the United States Of America

CONTENTS

PART 4: TURNS IN THE JOURNEY

PART 5: THE JOURNEY'S LEAD TO WHOLENESS

PART 6: SCRIPTURES FOR FREEDOM AND HEALING

PART 7: AFFIRMATION, DECLARATION, AND DECREE

ACKNOWLEDGMENTS

First, I would like to thank my Lord and Savior Jesus Christ for choosing me to live and survive the events recorded in this book and preordained by Him to reach the expected end of victory. I am humbled that He has trusted me enough to endure the hardships of life, learn, grow, and bring glory to Him.

Second, I thank everyone who challenged me to a painful or pleasurable change, especially those who were not afraid to tell me the truth in order for me to grow. Special thanks to my family and friends who have supported me as I have gone from an ugly caterpillar to a beautiful butterfly. I thank my angel, big sister & friend Cynthia McNeal (Stinker), who had seen greatness in me before it was ever manifested and had planted the right seeds that would one day take root.

To my precious, most loving, and caring God Mother, Shawna McKeither Burnett, and her family, for loving me through the worse chapters of my life since my childhood. They knew, despite what the outward demonstrated, that I was chosen by God and was beautiful inward and out.

I especially thank my dear friend and mentee, Rasheeda Clark (aka) Missy, for always pulling on my gift to teach and offer insight and sound wisdom from my experience and personal relationship with God. She constantly encourages me to write, write, and write so others will have the opportunity to be free and become whole through my voice, always demonstrating that my labor of love is not in vain. Finally, I am grateful to my

"Each day is an opportunity to change tomorrow because yesterday remains the same and can't be undone." —Unknown

wonderful parents who did their best in raising me and making sure my faith was rooted in the Lord Jesus Christ.

"But He was wounded for our transgressions, He was bruised for our guilt *and* iniquities; the chastisement [needful to obtain] peace *and* well-being for us was upon Him, and with the stripes [that wounded] Him we are healed *and* made whole." (Isaiah 53:5)

INTRODUCTION

"One thing I do [it is my one aspiration]: forgetting what lies behind and straining forward to what lies ahead, I press on toward the goal to win the [supreme and heavenly] prize." (Philippians 3:13–14)

Take a moment and put your best high-heel shoes on and accompany me on a journey to a life of liberty and wholeness. With each step we take throughout this book, we'll discover what holds us captive, and where we're hurting and why. We will travel through passages and take roads that will lead us from one stage to another. Throughout the journey, we will be progressed from captivity or restraint towards freedom. We will be empowered to bring conclusions to conflict and hurt from others, and ourselves.

We will be taken on a voyage to discovery, wherein we can accurately depict the lies we have long believed. We will realize that we can tap into the life we had envisioned when we refuse to allow any evidence of the outer world to distract us from becoming the person we were destined to be. This journey will restore us to having self- control and enable us to set boundaries no one can cross without our permission.

FOREWORD

This book is phenomenal, anointed, and power packed. I have known Apostle Free Hill for many years, while visiting the city of Philadelphia. I have watched the power of God, through the aid of the Holy Spirit and my ministry, tremendously transform her life. It is my belief that the Holy Spirit took her through the process, birthed her purpose through pain, and brought her into promise. As you read *When Your Heels Need to Be Healed*, you will feel her heart, soul, and spirit in the written words. This book is for everyone, especially those who are in need of a deeper or inner soul healing. I highly recommend and endorse this book, even for persons who haven't experienced this level of hurt—it will prepare them for their journey ahead. I am in agreement with Apostle Free Hill's advice, "In order to move forward we must destroy the past, don't leave it behind."

Shalom!

—Prophetess Miriam R. Emmanuel
Pastor of Good Samaritan Kingdom Ministries
and C.E.O/Founder of Miriam Emmanuel Network of Ministries
P.O. Box -N9308 Nassau N.P. Bahamas

APOSTLE FREE HILL

1

From the Heart & Mind of Liberty

"For whatever a man sows, that and that only is what he will reap." (Galatians 6:7)

Often times in life we are faced with the very same challenges, obstacles, and unfortunate circumstances. Yet they have entirely different outcomes and various effects. As individuals, we must take the necessary time to discover how each negative experience has taken a toll on us. We should not ignore feelings that are a result of what we've been through. We should not disregard, as well, the resentment we may harbor towards others whom we consider responsible for our pain. We must also be careful not to impose our thoughts, feelings, or decisions on others with whom we are in relation, expecting them to take on our internal burdens.

Rather, we must learn to openly discuss our feelings, and honestly articulate the defects we believe are in our lives because of others. Putting up a front or wearing mask only hurts more as it delays the process to liberation and healing. It also prohibits forward progression to having healthy emotions and relationships with people.

We are responsible for ourselves and do make final decisions on how life ultimately turns out for us. We determine whether to be victims of our past by living in the chains of pain, or take the initiative to destroy the yokes of bondage by looking at our past in the face rather than hiding behind it. Although the effects of life differ, the fact remains the same, whether positive or negative, our lives presently exhibit how we were influenced.

We must keep in mind that what we go through in life will assume our character and attitude in life. It will shape how we react or respond to life, with the understanding that past or present encounters and experiences can move or disturb us emotionally and psychologically. Therefore, it is vital we don't leave any form of negative impact unresolved.

PART 1

UNDERSTANDING THE JOURNEY

2

The Process

"He who looks carefully into the faultless law, the [law] of liberty, and is faithful to it and perseveres in looking into it... he shall be blessed in his doing (his life of obedience)."
(James 1:25)

The journey to freedom and wholeness can take days, months, years, or even seconds or minutes depending on what one desires and needs to be healed or liberated from. For the person's circumstances and situations, the process varies based on the degree of bondage, depth of pain, and the length of time in which one has been captivated.

The first step to be healed and liberated is the *recognition* that one is in some form of bondage or pain; whether it is emotional, physical, psychological, or spiritual. After acknowledging the need for healing and freedom, one must *identify* what he/she needs to be healed from, and make a conscious *decision* that they are willing and ready to take the necessary steps to reach what they desire.

The central focus has to be of self-taking a good look in the mirror. It is necessary to be truthful about what you like and dislike, your hidden pain, oppressed feelings, events that have transpired you, and people who have violated you. You need to be aware of those you feel are responsible for the hurtful things you've suffered. You must identify the secrets that you rehearse in your mind and are associated with present encounters that control your emotions and prohibit healthy relationships. One has to be willing to revisit hurtful places and peoples. This does not always relate to a physical interaction, although psychologically, emotionally, and verbally it is vital to the process.

Confrontation is healthy in this case. It provides an opportunity for one to be heard, relieved, and empowered to take steps toward freedom. Expressively communicating one's thoughts, feelings, or side of the story builds confidence, which is needed to face the real giants that are holding them captive.

sert chapter two text here. Insert chapter two text here.

3

The Temptation

"The man of many friends [a friend of all the world] will prove himself a bad friend, but there is a friend who sticks closer than a brother." (Proverbs 18:24)

Often times throughout life we *create* a world of our own that excludes what we've been through by blocking out facts. We try our best to *forget* everything negative that has taken place. We *attempt* to live positively by pretending we have it all together, we *feel* good about ourselves, and we *think* we are on our way to living our dream life. We *separate* ourselves from the people we love because realistically they play a major role in the pain we hide behind our smile. Therefore, we *form* families and relationships with people we meet as we rely on them to fill the emotional and void affection we lack because we have parted from our dysfunctional families.

By doing so, we set ourselves up for disappointment for we have made others responsible to play a role in our lives for which they were never intended, and often fall short of. We adopt play moms, turn our boyfriends into dads, and make our friends out to be siblings, only to find out later they are not whom we imagined them to be.

Our relationships are built on our true need for love and affection that we didn't receive from those who were responsible for giving it to us. This causes every other relationship to be an illusion or fantasy of what wasn't true. We can't continue to live as though we are okay with what happened or didn't happen for us when the truth is that we were affected in some form or fashion and have not gotten over it. We continue to oppress reality and are controlled in many areas of our life by it, hindering us from living free and true to ourselves and devaluing who we truly are.

4

The Way Out

"Happy (blessed, fortunate, enviable) is the man who finds skillful and godly Wisdom, and the man who gets understanding [drawing it forth from God's Word and life's experiences]." (Proverbs 3:13)

We must begin to accept our background and experience for what they are. For example, not everyone comes from two-parent homes with loving siblings and extended family members. Many of us grew up in single-parent homes and don't know the slightest thing about our absent-parent family. Some had both parents who only repeated how they were raised and growing up as children by parents that were bond by generational traditions and ways of doing things. Others have experienced sibling rivalry, parent's comparison, favoritism, and being identified as the "bad child" because you weren't afraid to express a different point of view or how you felt about things.

Maybe you were bold and verbal, yet your sibling was closed in and fearful, which was most likely the preference for others who looked upon your sibling as the "obeying" child. Never being properly interpreted, your sibling only goes with the flow of things out of fear because he or she witnesses the way you're treated when you were different. Or maybe, just maybe, that's their personality; meek and quite. Either way, there should be no differences in the love and acceptance of any child.

The way we are cared for and nurtured as children will determine the manner in which we conduct ourselves as adults. Whatever we are exposed and subjected to will, somewhere down the line, manifest itself negatively or positively in our lives. Nevertheless, the ultimate decision of the power it has, to dictate or control any part of our lives, is up to us. We must decide what to keep and what to put out with the trash!

There is no need to point the finger or blame anyone for our present state. The truth is that we are now responsible for our lives and where they are headed. Taking a good look into our souls can assist in making necessary changes towards a better life. Honesty is the key to unlock liberty in all aspects of humanity and can sometimes be painful yet worthwhile.

Remember, it may be true that we were mistreated, abused, neglected, abandoned, misunderstood, lied to, deceived, hurt, and some even left for dead. However, we don't have to become any of these things, nor do we have to treat others in such a manner.

Unbelievably, *the pain of your past has the power to produce a better tomorrow.* For example, I was raised in a strict "Christian" household where everything was dictated by my father. I had no voice and his discipline was child abuse. I was held captive living a life that consisted of going to every church service and attending school with a limited social life.

I didn't understand how serving God could be so miserable, mean, and set apart from family with no friends unless they were a part of the church. I couldn't understand why God didn't want to hear what I had to say or why He wasn't concerned about the way I felt. So I ran away from home, church, and everything familiar to me because I couldn't bear any longer the emotional, psychological, or physical pain I was going through. Of course, there is more to the story but you'll have to continue reading this book for more details.

5

On the Right Path

"Discipline your son while there is hope, but do not [indulge your angry resentments by undue chastisements and] set yourself to his ruin." (Proverbs 19:18)

After some time, I got to know God for myself and discovered that my parents were under strict religious leadership and ran their household accordingly. Most of their rules and traditions had nothing to do with God but were religious practices that bond me up as a person and had everything to do with parental fear. They feared that if they were not as strict and harsh with me, I would mess up my life by not trusting God. However, if they had taught me how to have a relationship with God and instilled Christian values in me, I would have made the right choices. Being raised in this kind of environment caused me to seek God for myself, build a personal relationship with Him, and know for certain what He requires of me.

I ended up having three children of my own who consider me to be the best mom. I built relationships with my children, I model to them leadership not dictatorship, I listen to what they have to say and in return they respect what I tell them. I give them room to fall short in order to learn and grow. I correct them then restore them back to the right road they should go.

I'm not the perfect parent by far but I didn't do what my parents did to me and the results as a mother have been great. I used to tell myself, "I'm not going to be like my parents when I have children. They were not aware of the damage they caused me or the hurt I endured and the resentment I had towards them." My parents had no idea who I was because they didn't know me personally. They only controlled me as their child and provided for me. Needless to say, that past pain empowered me as a mother. Later, I will share more about the positive impact some of my childhood pain had on me as a parent.

WHEN YOUR HEELS NEED TO BE HEALED

PART 2

THE JOURNEY WITH ITS

IMPACT

6

Sweet and Bitter

"Shall we accept [only] good at the hand of God and shall we not accept [also] misfortune and what is of a bad nature?" (Job 2:10)

I want to share the journey and its impact of when I became a wife. There is a whole other story of how my pain differently affected each of my relationships. I thank God I had the guts to look in the mirror of my soul, face the truth, and become whole.

Throughout my journey to freedom and wholeness, I discovered that sweet and bitter actually go well together. This happens once you figure out the perfect balance between the two and how to make it work for you.

Some brilliant chefs combine sweet and sour to create a sauce that tastes great on chicken or food of choice. Let's not forget about that magnificent person who mixes sweet and sour to produce those chewy sour patch candies we love. What about the bakers who mix the best cake icing using bitter and sweet ingredients?! How about the personality type that's straight forward yet meek, not to mention the beautiful runway models that combine sexy with sheik?!

As individuals, we must find balance. Although we prefer to have everything sweet, that's not realistic. The truth is that in order to grow, develop, mature, and appreciate life it takes sour. It's like eating something for the first time and having an allergic reaction so you're aware of what your body doesn't agree with. Like being born into poverty with the abilities and gifts to become rich. *Life doesn't come with a manual.* Although others teach us how to live, personal experiences have a way of differently teaching and shaping us. Sweet, as well as, bitter life experiences can teach you how to be proud of yourself without possessing pride, how to stand up for what you believe, and how to sometimes just enjoy the ride.

I know we all have heard the saying, "hurt people hurt people." Personally, I have found this to be true in my own actions towards others, and in the way others have treated me as a result of what they've been through themselves. When we unintentionally hurt or offend others, they have no idea we didn't intend it. So the only thing they can feel is the pain we caused.

APOSTLE FREE HILL

7

Marriage

"We as well as you once lived and conducted ourselves in the passions of our flesh [our behavior governed by our corrupt and sensual nature], obeying the impulses of the flesh and the thoughts of the mind [our cravings dictated by our senses and our dark imaginings]." (Ephesians 2:3)

T he following few pages are excerpts from my book *Wife vs. Helpmate*. It is to assist you in understanding how detrimental our past can be when we enter into relationships with these unresolved issues of the heart and soul, and how damaging we can be to someone else that we attempt to become one with.

Destroy your past. Don't "leave it behind!" Anything left behind can show up or be retrieved at a later time. Some of the very obstacles we face in our present relationships are from "leaving the past behind," never confronting it. In our marriages, our past begins confronting our spouses, who don't have a clue what has happened. When we ignore past experiences, pretending that hurtful things were not done to us, or acting as if we don't care about what people have done, we cause ourselves to become stagnated in our present state. This creates hindrances in pursuing our expected end. Everyone has a past, whether good or bad, and we can allow it to help us move forward in greatness or hurt us in remaining in the current state of abuse, rejection, and inward abandonment. The truth is that we proceed with the cares of life necessary to survive, but never achieve the success necessary for abundant life.

We, as wives, sometimes don't realize why we can't get ahead in relationships, ministry, workplace, or obtain the dreams and visions that are inside of us. The majority of our present struggles are associated with our past experiences and adversities. "Sweeping things under the rug" or hiding them in the closet won't bring closure. The word *past* is defined according to *dictionary.com* as, "The former part of someone's life kept secret or thought of to be shameful."

Once we give our hearts to Christ, there is no need

to be ashamed of our past or keep it in secret. Romans 8:1 assures us, "Therefore, [there is] now no condemnation (no adjudging guilty of wrong) for those who are in Christ Jesus, *who live [and] walk not after the dictates of the flesh, but after the dictates of the Spirit.*" Now if we are still allowing our past to control us, or condemn us and make us ashamed, maybe it's because we continue participating in past experiences. Remember that the above verse states that there is no condemnation when we walk not after the dictates of the flesh but after the Spirit. If our flesh is continuing to control us, we condemn our own selves.

Perhaps my experience will assist you in understanding. Before I accepted Christ as Savior and Lord of my life, and before I married my wonderful spouse, I was physically abused, neglected, rejected, abandoned, and misunderstood as a child. I was bossed around by my father and didn't have a voice or point of view about anything. What daddy said went, and there was no room for adjustment.

I witnessed my dad cheat on my mom, abuse her, be addicted to drugs and alcohol, yet he was a good provider and always around. When I became a born again Christian, I never dealt with the way I was treated and didn't realize how much my character, personality, and life were affected by it. When I married my husband, I was dominating him, wanted things my own way or no way. I would not allow him to have a say in decisions I made in the household. I was un-submissive, short-tempered, insecure, angry, religious, and would even strike him physically if I became angry enough. Although these behaviors were a result of what was done to me in the past, they dictated my actions in the present because I was controlled by my flesh and not by the Spirit of Christ. I did not have the character of Christ.

8

The Flesh or the Spirit

"But now in Christ Jesus, you who once were [so] far away, through (by, in) the blood of Christ have been brought near." (Ephesians 2:13)

Yes, we have Christ's Spirit in us but we must yield to Him. The flesh was able to overtake me in those areas because I did not make a choice to deal with my past experiences. I had not gotten intimate with God in my relationship with Him so that He would take me through the journey of deliverance and healing. I was attending a church where as long as the religious acts were done then you were considered saved and in right standing with God. This includes, for instance, showing up at every service, joining in all the good works and activities, and making yourself useful so the church could go on. This is was not for the purpose of growing and transforming into what God has called you to be.

I knew church activates, works, practices, and

behaviors but I did not know how to build my relationship with God until I realized it was not about the external but internal work. I needed Him to work in me. For years, I was unaware that the behaviors I exemplified were done to me out of ignorance by someone I loved dearly. I had taken on the characteristics of my experiences and couldn't see my potential to be a helpmate, not just a wife, or to understand what my role requires of me. Anything I felt in my flesh I would adhere to it, never considering the consequences. I would feel bad afterwards but would always find a way to justify my fleshly actions so I would not feel guilty.

I soon was illuminated by the Holy Spirit that the reason I continued with this behavior was because of ignorance in regards to deliverance and the need for it after my new birth. I was never taught how to confront my past and myself. I was not taught how to look at myself internally, opposed to focusing on my external position. I was bound and needed much deliverance and healing before I could become whole and the helpmate God promised my spouse. I had a love and a desire to please God and I longed to be like Him. I just didn't know how.

9

Temporary Change or Eternal Transformation

"Do not be conformed to this world (this age), [fashioned after and adapted to its external, superficial customs], but be transformed (changed) by the [entire] renewal of your mind [by its new ideals and its new attitude], so that you may prove [for yourselves] what is the good and acceptable and perfect will of God, even the thing which is good and acceptable and perfect [in His sight for you]."
(Romans 12:2)

The church taught me how to stop indulging in sin that others could see like, smoking, drinking, getting high, clubbing, and having children outside of wedlock. However, they never taught me how to become free of my internal struggles that no one can see like anger, bitterness, resentment, rage, rejection, low self-esteem, and insecurity. The church had no problem rebuking my behavior but they did not know how to set me free from the causes. That is because the church that I attended at the time was religious, and only knew how to address those external things, which would only result in temporary change. *I needed someone to address my internal turmoil for an eternal change.*

John 3:21 indicates, "But he who practices truth [who does what is right] comes out into the Light; so that his works may be plainly shown to be what they are— wrought with God [divinely prompted, done with God's help, in dependence upon Him]. For the first three years of my marriage, I hid behind church, my spiritual gifts, my prayer life, how much I knew the word of God, and my ability to dissect the Scriptures and interpret the divine will of God. I never realize that I was far from the woman and helpmate that God ordained me to be. Yet I learned how to operate and function with some of my gifts. The more time I spent with God, the more He revealed my areas of bondage. These areas were causing me to fall short of God's glory. They would have severed my relationship with my husband and best friend if I did not allow God to deliver and heal me of my past abuse, neglect, disappointments, and present religious bondage.

10

External Change or Internal Transformation

"Strip yourselves of your former nature [put off and discard your old unrenewed self] which characterized your previous manner of life and becomes corrupt through lusts and desires that spring from delusion." (Ephesians 4:22)

It was not until after I went through major deliverance and healing that the word of God began to take root in my life and internal transformation began to take place. In my time of prayer, I used to cry out to God about all the religious acts that my husband was not being participating in; like going to every church services, reading and studying his Bible, praying consistently, and actively participating in ministry. I was doing these things. But every time I hit the floor to tell God about my husband, God would in return tell me about myself. He showed me how I was using my ministry in the church as an antidote to cope with pain, rejection, and confusion. He revealed to me how I was hurting so bad on the inside. Although I was seeking after God, He showed me why I did feel so bad and acted so unseemly at times. Why when my soul was burning to be like God and to please Him, I would keep failing and disappointing Him by my actions.

As I continued to seek God through intense prayer and crying out to Him, He would show me my broken heart and the pain I endured as a child, which was hiding my potential and preventing me from going through the process for change. It hurt me so bad to see how my true character was, despite the church mask. I became so convicted that I needed to fast and pray for my deliverance. Then my prayer life shifted from a time of pointing out my husband's flaws, to a time of reflecting on myself, by examining my heart, and receiving direction from God as to becoming like Jesus. I finally took responsibility for my actions and stopped making excuses or blaming others for their actions towards me that provoked such ungodliness.

When I began to focus on myself, God took me to His word to show me that His Son already went through all that I suffered yet was without sin. He taught me that in order to be the great woman of God, I had to be delivered from the oppression of my past, be healed, and take on the true character of Christ. I needed to rid myself from the religious works that have a form of Christ but denying His power. When I began the journey, I saw my husband changing right before my eyes.

APOSTLE FREE HILL

11

The Change and Its Fruit

"If then you have been raised with Christ [to a new life, thus sharing His resurrection from the dead], aim at and seek the [rich, eternal treasures] that are above, where Christ is, seated at the right hand of God." (Colossians 3:1)

I had to study the Scripture to learn about those spirits I was imprisoned by, and to know how they gained access to my life and operated. I needed to know what triggered their manifestation, and how to cast them out of me. I needed to renounce and denounce them in my life in Jesus's name. I spent hours in prayer and studying the word of God along with reading books on deliverance, defeating darkness, and becoming a woman after God's heart.

My family and I stopped attending the church we were at, and got under a leader who dealt with the total man and had a deliverance ministry within the church. After joining the new church, I was baptized by the Holy Spirit with the evidence of speaking in tongues, which was something I was taught in error about. I truly went from religion to relationship and was able to identify the difference.

My prayer life changed dramatically because I learned so much, during the time I spent with God, about strategies and tactics against the enemy in prayer. I would decree the word of God over my life and see God act according to it. I was filled with such love, humility, and power that I was in awe watching my life and family change.

These experiences caused me to seek out God in ways I never knew existed. He taught me how to seek Him out in my intimate time with Him. I would travel near and far to learn and be imparted to know God without limits.

I became able to resist the anger and rage from my past. I even waged war against darkness, rejection, abandonment, and misunderstandings. My past experiences became the mirror to search my heart and check my character. I wanted to make certain that I wasn't the cause for people presently treating me in such a manner.

The control and insecurities turned into total

surrender, reliance, and trust in God. This resulted in humility and submission. The low self-esteem was transformed by a renewed mind. I came to understand that I was fearfully and wonderfully made by God, that I was royal, peculiar, and chosen. I realized that before I was formed in my mother's womb, God had already handpicked and ordained me to be great in Him. Everything the enemy meant for bad God began turning it around for my good. That was just the beginning of becoming a helpmate, suitable for my spouse, and a vessel of honor unto God.

Once I dealt with my past, God began changing my present, and preparing me for my future. Every time the enemy would try to oppress me with past temptations of the flesh, I would declare the word of the Lord in 2 Corinthians 5:17, which reads, "Therefore if any person is [ingrafted] in Christ (the Messiah) he is a new creation (a new creature altogether); the old [previous moral and spiritual condition] has passed away. Behold, the fresh and new has come!" I resisted the devil with the word of God, by taking on the character of Christ, and being set apart for God's use.

Wives, we don't have to be embarrassed or hide from what was done to us, even after we became born again. We don't have to keep skeletons in the closet or sweep our dirt under the rug and pretend that challenging events and circumstances didn't take place in our lives.

Often times we take on new roles that can bring about stress, difficulties, and challenge our characters. As a result, we put on a display over our troubled hearts to keep them hidden from others.

12

Moving Forward

*"For we are God's [own] handiwork (His workmanship),
recreated in Christ Jesus, [born anew] that we may do
those good works which God predestined (planned
beforehand) for us [taking paths which He prepared ahead
of time], that we should walk in them [living the good life
which He prearranged and made ready for us to live]."*
(Ephesians 2:10)

Whom the Lord loves He disciplines and corrects (see Hebrews 12:6). God will not allow His chosen vessels to remain bound by their past, or victims of present torment. He promised that we are more than conquerors through Him (Romans 8:37). He instructs us on how to overthrow the enemies' plans for our demise (see 2 Corinthians 10:5).

We must grow in our walk with God to a place where we can hear Him giving us instructions and showing us the areas that need immediate attention so we can be vessels of honor. When God allows us to go through the fire, it's to purify us so that we become more and more like Him in all aspects of our lives.

Wives, we must also have the ability to identify when it's time to move forward from one place to the other even in ministry. I am by no means suggesting to be a church hopper or unsettled. However, if you're not being challenged to grow in God and take on His character it may be the time for you to move forward.

God desires us to prosper and be in good health even as our souls prosper. He wants us to go from faith to faith and glory to glory according to His word (Romans 1:17; 2 Corinthians 3:18). If you are personally facing challenges seek wise counsel, or even professional assistance outside of the church. Don't give the enemy a foothold in your life by not attending to areas that don't represent God.

We are instructed by God to lay aside every sin and weight that so easily beset us, and to work out our salvation with fear and trembling (Hebrews 12:1; Philippians 2:12). Before we can be the best helpmate to our spouses, we must first become the best woman to ourselves. It is never too late for God to begin a new work on you as a wife, no matter how many years you have been married.

Now, fourteen years later I am a true woman of God, healed, delivered, a suitable helpmate, and adaptable to my spouse. What I recognized through my journey as a wife was that, not only my husband experienced my turmoil, my children did too, and everyone else with whom I had a relationship. Although each relationship didn't go through the extent my hubby had reached. Yet for any exposure to my past, to be subjected, it had to be difficult for others.

PART 3

HURT IN THE JOURNEY

13

Exposing My Past

"I do not consider, brethren, that I have captured and made it my own [yet]; but one thing I do [it is my one aspiration]: forgetting what lies behind and straining forward to what lies ahead." (Philippians 3:13)

L et's take a look at me for a bit. From what my mother tells me, I had been the type of child who knew what I wanted. I didn't settle for any answer or directive without an explanation. She expressed that I would ask numerous questions and always wanted to know who, what, where, how, and why. She said, although I wasn't the oldest, I took the initiative and led as the oldest child, never backing down. I didn't have a problem expressing how I felt even if it meant I would be reprimanded. My mother said I told the truth about everything. Even when I did wrong, I'd tell it myself. I was strong willed, bold, and never afraid.

Always concerned about others and standing up for them, I didn't like for others to be picked on, bullied or taken advantage of. When people would share what they felt about an individual or situation, I would be the one who spoke up when everyone else was afraid to do so. I was never a troublemaker and often times stayed by myself until someone else inquired some type of interaction. I was very observant of people and watched everything. When I didn't agree with something I made it known.

I can remember growing up desiring to be a lawyer and my mother would always tell me I would make a great lawyer because I was argumentative and confrontational with a strong desire to prove what I said was true. In the courtroom, that would have benefit me a great deal and would have been considered a strength. As a child, however, I was told that it was wrong, out of line, and I needed to shut up. Instead of my parents cultivating these strengths and teaching me how to use them with discipline and grace, they tried so hard to shut them down and make me act the way they thought a child should. Because my parents disagreed with the way I was, it made me reject myself.

I began thinking something was wrong with me

because I wasn't like my other siblings who just did what they were told despite how they may have felt. My parents basically raised us with the same rules, regulations, and disciplines with which they were raised. So from their perspective, they were great parents. They provided for us, were always at home with us, took us to church, and made sure we had what they considered a stable home.

As you can see, my parents' reality was quite different from mine. Often times I wished they'd give us a survey to know how we felt about what they were doing as parents, or how things were in the household in general. The sad thing is, they didn't care to hear how we felt good or bad, nor to understand our perspective on things.

As I mentioned earlier, I always expressed what I felt no matter what the consequences might be. I had an undisciplined tongue, as a result of never being able to express myself verbally without being disciplined or scolded as a child. I guess you can imagine that I grew into an adult with this same disadvantage. I would speak the truth in an offensive manner, my tone would often be loud, and I didn't consider the feelings of others just as long as I could say what I needed.

I didn't bother people but when they did me wrong

or hurt those close to me, I would treat them in such a harsh manner. I never realized that my responses were coming from a hidden place within where I suppressed rage and all the things I couldn't express in my childhood to people who hurt and offended me. Therefore, I didn't think before I spoke. I didn't count to ten and give an acceptable response. Instead, I reacted aggressively and defensively. I had no self-control.

When I became born again Christian, I knew this behavior was not good but I had no idea how to change it. I was certain I no longer wanted to respond to people or situations with this kind of temperament. I felt like I had no control over the way I reacted to negative confrontations.

I'll never forget being at a place of change and growth where so many things were lining up in my life for the better. As an individual, my character was transforming as I pursued God and sought to be more like Him by taking on His nature and possessing His attributes.

14

A True Test

"When swelling and pride come, then emptiness and shame come also, but with the humble (those who are lowly, who have been pruned or chiseled by trial, and renounce self) are skillful and godly Wisdom and soundness." (Proverbs 11:2)

Later, a situation arose between a few family members and myself. At this season in my life, I was not expecting anything negative from family members because I was changing. I was no longer the person they knew and with whom grew up. I barely interacted with them. To my surprise, however, two of my cousins called me; one was the mediator and the other had an offense towards me of which I was unaware. The true test started when the mediating cousin explained the reason for the phone call. My cousin, who held offense in her heart against me for something that transpired when we were younger, began to explain her feelings towards me. She stated that I offended her because I just said what I wanted when I wanted and didn't care if I hurt people's feelings. At this point, I had so many mixed emotions and the fire was boiling in my belly. I wanted to share what is in my mind about the things I disliked about her. At the same time, my heart was hurting that I made her feel this way. I didn't know if I should be angry with the mediator or glad, because I discerned she wanted someone to confront me and at the same time wanted us to be at peace as cousins.

At this time, I really needed God to help me and He did. I swallowed up my pride and allowed tears to fall. I responded with grace that God gave to me. I apologized and thanked her for having the heart to tell me how I made her feel.

That was a life-changing encounter for me. I began to search within myself to discover why I react to people with such hostility when they offend or hurt me. Why I have no control over my actions. Why such harsh verbal responses to individuals.

15

Defense Mechanism

"So then, whatever you desire that others would do to and for you, even so do also to and for them." (Matthew 7:12)

As I turned to God in prayer, He took me down in memory lane where my dad used to scold me so harshly when I didn't live up to his standards. This was when I would be told to shut up as I was expressing how I felt or explaining my actions. Not to mention the abusive physical punishment called "discipline."

God pointed out that I had a childhood rage and resentment that was oppressing me and dictating the majority of my responses to anything that I found to be hurtful. I would react in such a manner because this is where I felt safe. I made this behavior my defense mechanism. It was my way of protecting myself from further hurt or damage yet damaging others. Oh, how I wept and cried out to God to heal me from such a pain. He instructed me to denounce and renounce all childhood rage and resentment towards my parents and all others that hurt me. He taught me to forgive so I could be set free and then the healing would began.

The World English Dictionary defines *denounce* as "announcing the termination of a thing" and *renounce* is defined as "to give up voluntarily by formal declaration." What I did understand about my journey to being free and healed was that I had to be ready. I also had to be willing to accept the facts of others, like in the case with my cousin, because although what she experienced and felt was real it was not what I intended.

Listening to her speak so negatively about past behaviors at a time when I had made so many positive changes in my life hurt to the core. I wanted to understand why she came to me now when the events she shared happened so long ago. The truth was that she loved me and didn't want to stay bitter and apart. I too had grown to a place where I could accept negative feedback and bring about positive change in my own life. I learned that even in telling the truth that might hurt, if delivered in love, it would heal.

In the past, I delivered the truth from a place of hurt. I didn't consider the way I administered it, often times causing rejection and separation from those I truly loved. We must remember that truth is the key to freedom and opens the door for healing. We cannot express how others may feel, nor can we ignore that we may have caused negative feelings in others towards ourselves, despite what our intentions were. We can never be afraid or avoid facing ourselves if we want to be free from all prohibitions.

Making excuses will only delay the process. Trying to justify our actions is an indication that we aren't ready to work on ourselves. Being free and healed is not always about what others have done to us. It also includes what we have done to others even if we have a legitimate reason. Freedom and healing is not predicated on who's right or wrong but who's willing to be accountable and take responsibility. Through my journey of freedom and healing, I came to the realization that I can only change myself. And in changing myself I am empowered to set boundaries that protect me against repeating the cycle of being mistreated by others.

16

Facing Rejection

"My grace (My favor and loving-kindness and mercy) is enough for you [sufficient against any danger and enables you to bear the trouble manfully]." (2 Corinthians 12:9)

Let's take a slight turn in our journey down the road of rejection, where you're not accepted but abandoned and expected to alter who you are to accommodate those around you. It is when you are left feeling like you're some kind of freak because your point of views and perspectives differ from others.

The fact that your style and preference may be peculiar to most, and not popular, may make you stick out like a sore thumb, or like someone with some sort of handicapped. It's like wearing stripes with poke-dots or white after Labor Day and no one does that because society says, "it's a no, no." Imagine having leprosy and everywhere you went people stared at you because you looked different from them.

Dictionary.com defines rejection as "discarding as useless or unsatisfactory; to refuse to accept; to cast out eject, vomit out." As I write on this topic I feel it was like yesterday, remembering how being made to feel such pain brings me chills.

Rejection is rooted in childhood. It's not something that just happens when we're adults and make the choice regarding those we consider to be associates, friends, and the like. We began experiencing rejection in the environment we were reared in by those that nurtured us. Whether intentional or unintentional, the pain of it resides in us and subjects us to continue encountering this treatment from others.

When people are rejected, they feel a need to prove themselves. They become extreme and overbearing. They don't respect the point of views of others. And they always feel a need to be right. Rejection causes insecurities and suspicions. It causes people to perceive they will be criticized or betrayed by others before experiencing it.

Sometimes people take on an anti-social demeanor

and withdraw themselves because they fear no one's going to like or understand their personality. People, who are bound by rejection, void love and suffer from the inability to love others or receive love. For some, rejection was rooted after conception because one parent or both didn't really want the child but took the chances of birthing it. Fathers, who don't play an active role in the life of children because they are no longer involved with the mother, are also responsible for bonding children with rejection.

Rejection steals individual confidence and the ability to believe in one self to accomplish personal goals or join others in completing theirs, although fully equipped to do so. When children are deprived of spending quality time with parents, for reasons like working extended hours or spending too much time outside the home with others, it causes the feeling of rejection.

Whenever a child suffers from physical abuse, they are confused and fearful. Their timid minds automatically think they're being rejected. Sexual abuse causes children to distrust. It causes them to have a difficult time opening up to others especially authoritative figures. This is because they have been violated and feel the hurt of rejection.

As we can see, rejection can have a major impact on

the demeanor and character of an individual who has been exposed and subjected to it. Personally, I was a product of a childhood filled with rejection. The only exposure I can't recall experiencing is sexual abuse. As an adult, I exemplified several of the prior behaviors including reacting with anger, the need to get my point across and say what I felt despite others' feelings, and the difficulties I had with trusting people. These all were a result of being oppressed with past rejection. There was no way for me to be free from this behavior until I discovered the driving force behind it.

Often times we address the actions, which only hits the surface, and in return witness repeated cycles. Unless the root of any pain is pulled up to die, it will continue to grow because others will water and nurture it. Any form of abuse, misuse, hurt, or pain was first planted in our lives as a seed. The more these things happened to us the more they took root in our bodies, emotions, and minds, springing forth as negative fruit and painting the wrong picture of who we truly are. The repetitive abuse and pain done to us by others is the way these seeds grow and produce fruit. This is the watering and nurturing I formally described.

17

Hurting Heels

"The integrity of the upright shall guide them, but the willful contrariness and crookedness of the treacherous shall destroy them." (Proverbs 11:3)

Y ou can imagine my heels were really hurting now but life must go on, right? Wrong! What we must understand about leaving our heels hurting and continuing walking through life is that by doing so we cause the pain to become more intense and eventually we damage ourselves further. When the tap of your heels are worn down or broken, they can be replaced. But when the heel comes off, you must purchase a new pair of shoes. I went throughout life wearing down the taps on my heels continuously replacing them with people, places, things, and even God.

I found myself encountering identical hurt and pain of my past. I was so internally damaged that I tried to ease the pain with emotional eating, emotional spending, and emotional relationships, which resulted in becoming obese, broken, misused, and disappointed. My feelings dictated my life. I was always on an emotional roller coaster never finding inner peace or able to make sound decisions about anything. I reacted on impulse, often times being angry and filled with regret, suffering the consequences of my choices.

The relationships I had with others were unhealthy, because I needed to be accepted and loved. I clung to people who seemed to embrace me, who put forth effort to befriend me, and who showed interest. I loved people beyond measure. I fought for others. I gave up my time and substance to be sure they were happy. I accepted people as they were never pressuring me and I did expect them to be anything else. What I didn't know was that the depth of my love and desire to attach myself to others came from a place of rejection and all the pain I suffered from childhood.

My heels ran away from home by the age of fourteen with nowhere to live. Because I was too afraid of my dad's physical abuse, I did not go my relatives or anyone they knew. I was afraid he would find me or they may make me return home. I decided to rear off on to Wilderness Road where breaking free from bondage led me.

I can recall planning to leave home and never return after getting beaten on my bottom with a 2 x 4 stick for what seemed like hours. My dad had beaten me so long this time that I couldn't feel anything. All of my limbs were numb. My mother was too afraid herself to intervene.

I saved my lunch money up for a week so I could pay someone to take me home to get my clothes during school time and work hours. At the time I was in high school, I had close friends who knew my home life and how I was restricted. For some time, I lived from girlfriend's house to another until their moms were asking too many questions. I was able to stay with one of my best friends whose mom treated me as if I were her own. She raised concerns about whether or not my parents were aware how much time I was spending at her house. Of course, my best friend and I lied and told her, "Yes." As a mother, she knew within herself that something was wrong. She already knew that I came from a strict Christian home and my parents wouldn't be allowing such a thing all of a sudden. My best friend and I used a "little wisdom" where I would only come over after her mom went to bed so I would have a place to stay.

18

With A Boyfriend

"But sin, finding opportunity in the commandment [to express itself], got a hold on me and aroused and stimulated all kinds of forbidden desires (lust, covetousness)." (Romans 7:8)

My best friend had an older brother whom I began dating. When their mother found out, she approved because she loved me but was concerned because of my age. I started spending more time with her son, even spending the night with him, but she told both of us that we couldn't do that in her home. She explained to me that she loved me a lot and was concerned about me. She said that as a mom she wouldn't want someone to just allow her daughters to be at their home with their son not knowing what was going on. I understood but my boyfriend didn't. He was highly upset.

At the time, they lived in Frankford Housing

Development. They had an aunt who lived in the same complex and was a drug addict at the time. Because my boyfriend knew my predicament, and we thought we were in love, he asked her if we could stay in her house, which was a crack house. I didn't know what to do. I was afraid. I wanted to go home but I knew I couldn't. So I ended up living in the crack house with him.

His mom was really hurt to see us do that but there was nothing she could do. In our minds, we were together and that's all that mattered. My boyfriend was a few years older than I was. We hung out a lot and he hustled to take care of us. He was not a nonsense type of guy, with a short temper, and very charming. He was close with his family and took good care of them as well.

At this time, I was introduced to smoking marijuana and drinking. To some degree, this eased the pain I had. The reality is, although I was not at home where I thought I was being treated so badly, I was hurting and devastated because I missed my family, especially my five sisters I left behind. I cried every time I was alone mainly at night. He would try to comfort me and always asked if I wanted him to take me home because he wasn't afraid of my dad. My answers was always, "No."

Eventually he started leaving me in the crack house all day by myself while he ran the streets with his friends. He would make sure I had money and food then be on his way. We began arguing and fighting all the time because I would be very confrontational when he came in. I'll never forget our last fight. He thought he could slap me and run out the house because I was topless. Before I knew it, I was running through the crack house, out the door behind him. When he turned back to look and saw me running behind him topless, he took his shirt off and put it around me. We went back in the house and cried together. He was young and I was young. He said he didn't know what I wanted from him. He thought he was treating me well. I explained how I felt and we apologized to one another.

As time went on, he changed a little and I ended up pregnant. I was fifteen years old back then. We never went to the doctor but my stomach just kept growing. Although I was very small and able to hide it, I had no idea what to do. He, on the other hand, was happy and excited that I was devastated. I started hanging out the house more because I didn't want to inhale the fumes from the crack being smoked in the house.

Lo and behold, there were rumors that he was

messing around with another young woman whom he dealt with prior to me. I confronted him and, of course, he denied it all. Oh, to his surprise she came and told me herself that they were messing around. She was pregnant. When he came home, we argued back and forth and he kept lying. So far, I was able to put up with lots of things but cheating was not one of them. This is when I got the courage to go home. I packed up what I could and I left him.

19

Back Home

"I will get up and go to my father, and I will say to him, Father, I have sinned against heaven and in your sight."
(Luke 15:18)

I went home, knocked on my parents' door, and I could hear my sisters screaming, "She's back, she's back." My dad came and let me in. I believe, at that moment, he was so glad to know I was alive. He didn't know how to respond except to welcome me in. It was awkward, because I had been gone so long and my family wasn't good at communicating, that we didn't really talk about where I had been.

After being home for a while, my parents enrolled me back in school. At the time, they didn't know I was expecting a baby. As time went on and I kept gaining weight, my dad asked my mom if I was pregnant. My mom asked me when was my last menstrual and I told her I didn't know. She then made an appointment for me to see the doctor and found out I was almost six months pregnant.

I did not want my dad to find this out but my mom told him. I had never seen my dad speechless. I could see the hurt on his face and he didn't utter a word to me for the remainder of my pregnancy. He reported to the pastor at the church we attended and the pastor said I could not attend church pregnant. I was very upset that I was not welcomed in the church any longer. I already disliked the way people talked about others and looked down on those that weren't doing what they did. This just sent me over the edge.

I ended up going into premature labor and having my daughter at six and a half months. I was sixteen years old. I was not in contact with my daughter's father. I had no desire to interact with him because he hurt me to the core and betrayed my trust. Finally, one time he called after I had the baby and I answered the phone. I told him I had a baby girl and shared her name. He was good and bold. He came to my house and my dad told him that he better never come back again. That didn't stop him from trying. He kept calling and trying to come to see our daughter. I started sneaking my daughter to his house to see him. When no one was at home, I would allow him to come and see her. His family loved her dearly, especially his mom who was hurt because my dad wouldn't allow them to be a part of her life.

Not much had changed at home; same routine and state as it was before I left. I wanted to go places with my daughter but was always told, "No." I spent most of my days in my bedroom depressed. By the time my daughter was one, I was ready to leave again one day. I tried going out with my daughter but my dad scolded me, forbidding me to go out with her. He made it very painful that if I wanted to go out I was not allowed to take her with me.

APOSTLE FREE HILL

20

With Another Man

"These six things the Lord hates, indeed, seven are an abomination to Him... A heart that manufactures wicked thoughts and plans, feet that are swift in running to evil."
(Proverbs 6:16–18)

A t this time, I was attending a different high school with new friends and associates. I started a new relationship with a man who was very meek, humble, and laid back. He didn't have either of his parents in his life and lived with his aunt. We became very good friends and shared some of our most intimate secrets. We bonded in a different way. It was almost like we needed each other.

He met my daughter since he would walk me to my grand mom's house where she was while I was at school. We became intimate and didn't want to be a part from one another. We began cutting school to be together. I eventually left home again but this time I didn't just leave my family I abandoned my child. I left without her. I moved in with my boyfriend and his aunt and her children. She didn't care, as long as he gave her money anytime she'd ask. I didn't care for the way she treated him. She was controlling and manipulative and used the fact that he had nowhere to go to her advantage. She had multiple personalities and was addicted to medication and alcohol. She and her boyfriend fought all the time. She was verbally and physically abusive to her daughters, who actually bonded with me to some degree.

My heels have now turned down the same road. I was living with my teenage boyfriend and his family, missing my own. Yet this time my heart was broken because I couldn't stop yearning for my daughter. All I could remember was my dad telling me I couldn't run the streets with her. I knew there was no way of leaving the house with her. My teenage boyfriend was hustling to make money to care for us and make sure he paid his aunt. We both ended up dropping out of high school, doing nothing. I was in the tenth grade and he was in the eleventh.

While living with him I met some wonderful people

who lived across the street from him. It was a family who was originally from North Carolina, at least the wife was. She was about ten years older than I was and had a husband and two beautiful children. Her husband worked long hours to provide for the family. So she and I began to spend a lot of time together. I had never met anyone quite like her. She was loving, caring, a wonderful mother, and beautiful wife. She told me I had an old soul and couldn't believe my age. Each day, our relationship grew closer and closer. I shared the truth about my life with her and she felt really bad for me.

What I loved the most about her is that she didn't try to be my mother. Without knowing, she gave me what I desired from my mom. We grew as sisters and became inseparable. Her husband and children loved me as well. She took me to North Carolina to meet her family. The love they embraced me with was almost unreal. It was like the family I longed for.

My boyfriend, at the time, became close with her and the family as well. We were all like brothers and sisters. She knew the type of woman his aunt was because they were neighbors, and of course, we shared our experiences with her. I spent most of my time at my friend's house and went home when it was time for bed or when my boyfriend got home.

21

Stinker-Angel

"A friend loves at all times, and is born, as is a brother, for adversity." (Proverbs 17:17)

I am now nineteen years old, a high school dropout, living with boyfriend, having no contact with my biological family or daughter, and is now expecting my second child. When I shared with my sister-friend that I was pregnant, she just held me and we cried. She assured me that I would be okay. She began teaching me how to be a young woman and do the necessary things to care for myself. She encouraged my boyfriend and I to return back to school, but neither of us listened. She took me to apply for benefits for the baby and myself so I would have something of my own as a source of provision.

Things got really bad across the street at the house

of my boyfriend's aunt. She started to pick fights with us, asking for extra money and so forth. Being pregnant, this was way too much stress on me. We didn't have the money or the means to get a place of our own. My sister-friend knew what we were undergoing. So she with her husband decided we could move in with them. They were like angels sent from God to help me keep my sanity. No one knew that behind my smile and exuberant laughter my heart was torn to pieces, wishing I was at home with my own family.

My sister-friend's name was Cynthia but her country nickname was Stinker. So from here on out I will refer to her as "Stinker." I'm sharing her name because I know she wouldn't mind. I want everyone who reads this book to know the name of the woman God used to carry me through my young adult life and teach me how to survive. She is the woman who took the time to listen to how I felt, shared my pain with me, and to the best of her ability allowed her love to heal me to a place where I didn't give up on life.

Living with Stinker was such an awesome experience. I witnessed what a loving family looked like. I admired the loving relationship she had with her children and desired the same. She knew me so well that if I was quite she knew what it meant. She knew how to calm me down when I was angry. She always had my back even if I were wrong, but would correct me later. She was nurturing, sweet as honey, and fierce as a lion. Whatever she had I had. She never asked my boyfriend or me for anything the entire time we were with her and her family. She pushed me to at least after the baby take up a trade so I could further myself and one day reunite with my daughter and care for my own family. She was always uplifting and encouraging, telling me how beautiful and smart I was. She would always remind me of how genuine and loving my heart was. We weathered the storms together as sisters and friends. We knew we had a bond that would see no end. Stinker understood that I was hurting deep down on the inside. She did everything within her power to help me get through my days. Everyone in the neighborhood thought we were blood sisters. That's how close we grew. When they saw her, they saw me.

Stinker tried to get me to call my family and at least let them know that I was okay. She told me that they, especially my daughter, were missing me and hurting just as I were. Still, I just couldn't conqueror my fear and do it. Expecting a second child made it even more difficult. At night, I would pray and cry to God about how I felt. I can recall waking up every day with a headache and puffy eyes from crying. My boyfriend and I were still together although he was hanging out with his friends more. The further along I was in my pregnancy I had Stinker. Thank God!

WHEN YOUR HEELS NEED TO BE HEALED

PART 4

TURNS IN THE JOURNEY

22

A Painful Direction

"Lean on, trust in, and be confident in the Lord with all your heart and mind and do not rely on your own insight or understanding." (Proverbs 3:5)

Now my hurting heels would take a turn in a direction I never imagined taking. At this time, Stinker was in school studying for cosmetology. One day, her children were in school and my boyfriend was out and about. While I was at home alone, I went into labor. So I caught the bus to the hospital. After being evaluated and kept for hours, they were able to stop my labor. They gave me specific instructions and sent me home, for I was only eight months.

Once I got home and rested for a while, I had to go get a prescription filled that was given to me when I was released from the hospital. I decided to walk to the pharmacy, which was about five blocks away. As I was walking down the street, I heard the tires of a vehicle streaking and someone calling my name. When I turned to look, it was my mom and siblings.

My mother quickly pulled out of traffic and came running to me. She grabbed me and started to cry. All I could do was to cry myself. I knew at that moment that God answers prayers and was concerned about how hurt I really was. My mom started to ask me all kinds of questions. I explained to her that I was okay, went into false labor, and was going to get my prescription filled. She wanted so badly to take me home with her. But she as well as I, knew that this was not a good idea without consulting with my dad first. We stood there talking, hugging, and crying for a while. My siblings were so excited to see me just as I was to see them. My mother took me to the pharmacy and dropped me off at home. I promised her that I would keep in touch. She told me how much they missed me, especially my daughter. I could feel the pain she felt having to leave without me.

When everybody finally got home that day, I shared what happened. Of course, everyone wanted to know why I didn't call anyone when I went into labor. That must have been a trick question because they already knew that I was stubborn and liked to do what I could on my own. Stinker did warn me not to do it again. Everyone was so excited for me and wanted to know if I was going to see my family. I explained that I would start by calling and see how it goes from there.

As I promised, I remained in touch with my family and was able to talk to my daughter whom I hadn't seen or heard from for years. This was more difficult for me than not being in contact with them at all. Each time I spoke to one of them I would cry and so would they because we wanted so badly to be together. At this point in my life, I had journeyed so far from home that going back there was not what I desired to do, although I wanted to be with my family. I had grown into a young woman and suffered my way to be able to sustain in life without them. Yet, I knew I couldn't live by the rules and dictatorship at home. So there was no need for me to make an attempt to getting there.

23

A Happy Reconnection

"Through skillful and godly Wisdom is a house (a life, a home, a family) built, and by understanding it is established [on a sound and good foundation]." (Proverbs 24:3)

The following month, I had a healthy baby boy. I was very excited because my mother gave birth to six girls never having a son. I wanted her to finally be able to have a male child around. By this time, we had rebuilt a good relationship with my family. They even got my dad on board and ended up coming to the hospital to see me with the baby. This was one of the happiest days I had seen in years. My mom didn't want to leave. She just sat and held her grandson, kissing, and rocking him until visiting hours were over. It felt great to be connected to them again. I started visiting with them and they would visit me. Stinker and her family became close with my family and things were looking up for us.

My boyfriend and I finally moved out on our own about ten blocks from Stinker. Of course, I wasn't going to move too far from my sister. She and I still hung out every day. Either I would walk to her house for the exercise or she would pick me up when I didn't feel like it. She was the godmother of my son. I knew if, God forbid, anything happened to me or his father, she would love and raise him as if she gave birth to him.

My family were still faithful in church. My mom and dad were a Reverend and Evangelist at their church and were very involved. My mom started asking Stinker and I to come out to services they would have. We did go as we were attempting to live better lives.

After having my son, I knew I needed to do more. I wanted a better life. So I enrolled in school to become a Certified Nursing Assistant. I passed with an A in all classes. I even passed the states test with an A. Soon after completing the course, I got a decent job. I was working good hours and my son spent a lot of time at my parents' house. My dad kept my son with him most of the time. He would come pick him up even if I had nothing to do.

By making steps toward having a better life, I finally was able to give my parents a little something to be proud of me. Now that I was an adult living on my own, something that they would consider legit because I was of age, we could get along better. They chose to accept me the way I was. They had no choice because I was out on my own.

Although we were reconnected and moving forward there was still something missing. I wanted so badly to discuss all these years I had been gone. I wanted them to ask why I left the house. I didn't want those things bottled up on the inside of me. But like everything else, it went unaddressed. Moving these hurting heels right along with my parents showed that I was doing well enough to have my daughter back with me, who was now seven about to turn eight. That was the greatest news I could ever have gotten on this journey.

24

A Responsible Adult

"If you will turn (repent) and give heed to my reproof,
behold, I [Wisdom] will pour out my spirit upon you, I will
make my words known to you." (Proverbs 1:23)

Stinker decided to return to North Carolina and that I could move into the house. I had an efficiency at that time. The house was paid for and all I had to do was pay my own bills. What a blessing from God. Once again, my angle made sure I was set to continue on with life. This separation devastated both of us. We cried and cried because we didn't know what we would do without each other. I knew for certain that I had to be strong and become an even better person even now. That is because my role model was going on and now I had to put into action all she taught me. Having both of my children presented that opportunity for me in an even greater way.

My boyfriend had been arrested and we were no longer a couple. It was only my children and I. A time for me to be a responsible adult and care for my family. How did I end up with two children to care for with neither of their fathers is actively present in their lives? I wasn't what they call a fast girl. Getting into relationships with boys wasn't really my thing. Furthermore, my father made sure we would not talk with them. My mother was in total shock when she found out I was pregnant because she knew I wasn't kid friendly. The church viewed me as a fornicator and threw me out. There was no place for me amongst the religious neither did I make a place for myself around family and naysayers that spoke negative about me. They were making statements that I would never be anything, and all I would do is to keep having babies out of wedlock because I didn't like listening to anybody. The truth wasn't that I didn't like listening to anybody but that I needed to hear from somebody that understood, cared, and could relate to me as an individual. I needed guidance and those that were part of my life before didn't give me direction. Therefore, I had to figure things out with every turn of my heels through life's journey.

Now my heels seemed to be in a place of having some stability where many would consider a normal life, heading in the right direction. But that wasn't the case at all. The outward appeared to be normal but inwardly I was a total wreck. I was a mother of two children who depended upon me to love, provide, teach, and nurture them. I put my best heel forward and began my new life, raising my son and daughter. I worked hard daily to provide for them, brought them the best of everything, and made sure they did well in school. I spent long hours talking with them to make sure I knew how they felt about our lives together. Yet something was still missing.

My daughter was ecstatic about living with her brother and I because she lived with my parents for so long but always was desiring to be with me. She seemed distant from me, like we were not bonding or connecting in some way. I thought that maybe she missed my parents and siblings because they were all she knew. From my perspective, I was being the best mommy to my children. I had finally gotten to a place in my life where they were my first priority.

My children would spend the weekends over my parents' house and I would go out with my friends and party over the weekend. I was single for some time after my last relationship. I didn't want to have different men around my children, especially if they were not going to be committed. It seemed like every male that I met was just not what I anticipated to be a family man, or one that I could be serious with, or expose my children to. In all honesty, I wasn't sure about what I wanted in a man. But I was certain about what I didn't want. I did not want someone to tell me what to do, or who ran the streets and cannot provide, or someone who was dishonest.

25

Yet With Another Man

"The man of many friends [a friend of all the world] will prove himself a bad friend, but there is a friend who sticks closer than a brother." (Proverbs 18:24)

A s I continued on being single and raising my children, there was an emptiness in my life that I couldn't fill. I had plenty of friends, was well known and liked in my neighborhood, and all types of males were attracted to me. Finally, I decided to give dating a try. I met an extremely handsome man, charming, respectful, and caring. We were friends for a while before I allowed him to meet my children. As time went on, I learned more about his life but I wasn't too impressed. However, by now I found myself wanting him more instead of less.

He was good to my children and me. He worked as

a barber, was well known, and respected. He liked being popular in the street and had a temper hot like fire. I met his family and loved each of them. He had two daughters and a stepdaughter, from a prior relationship, that I absolutely adored. His children and my children were able to bond because they spent time at our house with us. Eventually, he moved in with me.

Here it goes again that these heels were living with another man. At least this time around it was in my own home. Nonetheless, it wasn't a good idea. Playing house is never a choice one should make. I was in pursuit of the structured household I grew up in with two parents and children, minus all the dysfunctions. We had well times together living like a family. But I didn't care for some of the indulgences that my new lover was in. I came to find out that the whole barber thing was just a cover up for a major hustler in my day. I wondered how he always had such an overflow of money. Of course, at the time I didn't ask too many questions as long as the home was taken care of.

I myself had a short temper and didn't tolerate much foolishness in my relationships, especially as I witnessed how my mother suffered at the hands of my father before he became born again. I did not have a nonsense mentality and was confrontational with the men with whom I found myself in relationships. We began arguing more than usual. He seemed to think it was okay to spend a substantial amount of time outdoors once he moved in and I shouldn't have a problem. That is because he thought it was okay since he was taking good care of the children and me. I started to get suspicious because he would sometimes stay out overnight and use "getting money" as a legitimate reason. He would get his children in the weekends and never be there with them, not that I mind the children, but I did mind him not being there to spend time with them.

I continued to work hard and be a mom. My children would hear us arguing because he was spiraling out of control with his street life. On numerous occasions, I discussed this behavior with him and was always promised that it was going to change. Nothing changed. The better things only got worse. I was tired and miserable but didn't have the heart to end the relationship. The arguing turned into pushing and shoving and had gotten more frequent. He liked to drink champagne and he would be like a mad man when he consumed too much.

26

When Confidence is Betrayed

"[My companion] has put forth his hands against those who were at peace with him; he has broken and profaned his agreement [of friendship and loyalty]." (Psalm 55:20)

He had finally struck a nerve when I heard a rumor that he had been fooling around with another young woman that I actually knew to be his "god-cousin." She is someone I suspected since I ran into her at his place of employment while she didn't have a son to get his hair cut. When I questioned, he gave some excuse that she just stopped by to check on him.

That gut feeling that he was lying was warning me all the while. Once again, here is a cheater who thought I could be deceived and wouldn't find out. This devastated me because I was a loyal girlfriend and respectful. I took care of all the domestics of the home, worked hard, and had this man's back no matter what. I felt betrayed, used, and mistreated by him. I confronted him and he denied ever having a relationship outside of ours. He insisted that I expose the person who told me. He knew that most of the guys in the neighborhood were afraid of him because of his temperament. I didn't tell him anything.

At this point, I told him I no longer wanted to be with him and he didn't want to hear it. He didn't move out the house and I left well enough alone. I allowed him to continue living with me and bringing me his money. I played along with him like I was still in love. But the truth is that I had emotionally left him and didn't care much about what he was doing outside the home with another woman. I lived my life and he lived his. Surprisingly he tried to spend more of his time at home because, of course, he was caught. It was too late and I had no interest in being with him. It was something about infidelity that I just couldn't bounce back from in a relationship.

I had learned from childhood how to be physically somewhere, but emotionally and psychologically leave in order to survive. When it came to relationships, I didn't think I could go through anything worse than what I endured at home. Just look at these heels in another relationship that gone bad. What's so sad about all three of them is that I was treated like a queen as if I were God's gift to men. It was like there was no other woman in the world to compare to, until commitment and loyalty were a requirement and anything outside of this I wasn't willing to tolerate. These men would build my confidence long enough to have me emotionally wrapped around them and then take it away from me when I wouldn't settle for the same in return.

Dictionary.com defines confidence as "full trust, belief in the powers, trustworthiness, or reliability of a person or thing." Emotionally and psychologically, this is just what these men gained from me. The reason is that I didn't have confidence in myself. I had no clue how to do this. *Dictionary.com* also describes confidence as "belief in oneself and one's power and abilities, self-confidence, self-reliance, assurance." I was unaware of my own power and abilities despite that I was caring for my children and myself at the time. All I knew was how to depend upon others to feel complete or valuable, because I was taught as a child to depend and rely solely upon my parents and to trust what they said even if I didn't agree.

Confidence in myself was not a characteristic I

possessed, which made me vulnerable to men who wanted me to need them and for different reasons they needed me. I continued repeating the same cycles and patterns in regards to my relationships and didn't know how to break free. My heart was aching so badly to the point where I didn't want to live anymore. Thoughts of suicide crossed my mind on several occasions but I didn't want to leave my children behind with no one to raise them right. I certainly didn't want them to be raised by the harsh hands that reared me up. The only hope that I could cling to was having my children with me every day. I was in so much emotional pain in this relationship that I couldn't think straight.

27

Exhausting Relationship

"Treasures of wickedness profit nothing, but righteousness (moral and spiritual rectitude in every area and relation) delivers from death." (Proverbs 10:2)

It hurt me daily to wake up to a man whom I couldn't trust. I was only continuing with him because I was an emotional wimp and couldn't pull myself to put him out and walk away. For peace sake, I allowed him to stay because I knew he was not leaving without a fight. Each passing day I became angrier at my circumstance. I was bitter, my attitude was nasty, and my patience was short. I lessened my interaction with my children. I lost my appetite and desire to get up and take care of activities of daily living. I began calling out of work, taking the children to school, and secluding myself in my bedroom until it was time to pick them up. I tried my best to hide what I was experiencing from my children. However, they could discern the hurt and had to encounter my inability to properly care for them when they called upon me.

My significant other could no longer receive any emotional or psychological support from me. I could no longer strike his ego. I was unable to domestically care for him. I stopped all sexual contact because of my lack of trust. At this point, the distance that I drew between us was too much for him to bare. So he drifted further away into the streets. This didn't bother me because I had no desire for him to be around my children and me anyhow. I wasn't good at responding to life circumstances in a healthy manner but I was great at reacting to pain despite the cost.

I would be lying if I said I didn't care about him, or deep down wanted him to change and be the man of my dreams. I would have even settled for the charm and good looks with which he swept me off my feet. That, however, was not happening. Instead, his behavior became more unattractive than it had ever been in our relationship. He was drinking too much. Every time he came home, he was intoxicated and started getting disrespectful verbally. I was accused of finding someone else and was being called out my name, which result in intense arguments.

At this point, the pain and pressure of this relationship was becoming too much. So I did the one thing that I knew would bring me some type of relief, which is to pray. Whenever I felt like my heels were going to break in my journey I would began crying out to God, expressing that I couldn't take anymore. Except this time, it was different for me. Not only could I not continue in the pain of my circumstances, but also I couldn't bare the pain that my heart was feeling from life altogether.

I felt as though I had lost all sanity and touch with reality. It felt like I was numb and walking around like a zombie. I felt paralyzed to life and my surroundings. I started to send my children to my parents' house more frequently because I couldn't cope well with my reality. My family knew something was wrong but nobody bothered to ask. I didn't have Stinker to rescue me from my despair. All I could do was to call upon the God in whom I was taught to believe. Day in and day out, I would cry and pray. I would express to God how I was feeling, and if He would rescue me I would never stop going to church again.

One early morning before sunset, I got a phone call from my significant other that would change my life forevermore. He called me in duress. Instead of doing what he instructed me to do, I went running to his rescue. To my surprise, things were much more serious than I expected and tragedy struck. I had never seen him this high and intoxicated, or angry before. I tried my best to calm him down and divert his attention from what was transpiring. I cohered him into leaving with me and returning home. Nothing I tried worked. This night broke the heels off my shoes and changed the direction of my life. Because of what happened this night, I spent almost two years questioned by police, afraid someone was going to kick my door in, and the sound of helicopters made me sick.

I watched this man in my life go from what society consider a ten to a zero in a matter of days. He would get so high where he couldn't function. He would be away from the house for days and call me to come get him scarcely knowing his whereabouts. I would figure it out from the landmarks he provided to go get him. When I found him, he would be outdoors sitting on the ground smelling like someone who hadn't bathed in weeks. I would just take him to the house, bathe him, and allow him to sleep for days but he would go out again.

As much as I thought I was done with him, I didn't dessert him. I was hurt seeing him in this state. The only thing that I could rehearse in my mind and emotions were the times he was good to my children and me. Therefore, I couldn't walk away from him now that he had nowhere to turn. I was furious with him because of the predicament we were now in because of his actions. But my heart wouldn't allow me to turn my back on him. He became more violent toward me. He was not in his right state of mind. I became threatened and knew there was no way for me to live together anymore. I began to ask him to gather his belongings and move out of my home but he would not budge. All I could do was to pray. I had no one to turn to but God.

I separated myself from my family who had reached out to me after the incident. I denied knowing what my parents were talking about when they came to find out what was going on, since they heard from a family member about what happened. I can remember crying out on the inside but it wouldn't come out of my mouth. I so badly just wanted my dad to act as he did when I was a child and make me go with him. I could tell by the look in his eyes that he knew I was being dishonest. Yet I felt as though there was nothing he could do.

28

A Birth and a New Birth

"Jesus answered him, I assure you, most solemnly I tell you, that unless a person is born again (anew, from above), he cannot ever see (know, be acquainted with, and experience) the kingdom of God." (John 3:3)

My significant other remained in the home with me and I continued suffering emotional and psychological abuse from him. Each day I thought my life was going to end. Because I was so afraid, I planned to have a child with him, thinking that if I had this child he would never hurt me again. As planned, I conceived and he was overwhelmingly happy and excited, especially when he found out it was a boy. This was such a stressful and painful pregnancy. The fighting between the two of us hadn't ceased.

I was passing blood clots of the size of the palm of

my hand. The doctors did not think that I would have the baby. My significant other attempted to do better but it was too far gone for him to make lasting changes. His life was destroyed. All the while, I never stopped praying to ask God to save me. I made a vow to God if He delivered me this time I would never choose a man over Him or turn my back on Him again.

In July of that year, I got a phone call from my mother, asking me to attend a service she was having at church called "Prodigal Son." By now, I was eight months pregnant and had no desire to visit the church that put me out during my first pregnancy. It was that church that talked so badly about me and looked down on me. I told my mother this very thing and she assured me that if I came, God was going to move in my life. She said that God told her to invite me. I told her that I would consider it. I knew I had nothing left to loose. Some church folks, who are looking down or talking badly about me, was the least of my worries.

I knew I needed God to intervene by way of miracle because there was no other way for me to make it in this life. I swallowed my fears and anxieties of being rejected, mistreated, and talked about. So I attended the service. I took my broken heels to the house of God on July 25, 1999. I walked down a long aisle with everyone, up to the second pew from the front, staring at me. I figured if I sat all the way in the front I wouldn't have to see all the whispering or mean faces and hands with knives that are behind me.

My mother preached about the child who left God and it was time for him to come home because God was waiting. Of course, I'm paraphrasing but that was the moral of the message. I cried the entire time she preached. I could feel God pulling my spirit and touching my heart, reassuring me that He had been waiting on me and heard my cry. This was the day I had been given a choice between life and death, a second chance, and an opportunity to be free despite the odds that were against me. What came to remembrance was a passage of Scripture I heard quoted as a child in church "If God before you who could be against you." It gave me strength.

When the altar call was given, I walked myself to the altar and cried unto the Lord. He answered me and I received the plan of salvation that day. I could feel a weight lifted from me although my circumstances at home hadn't changed. I wasn't the same and for once I had confidence to make the right decisions for my life. I knew without a doubt that there would be controversy at home. That is because I now would have to tell the father of my unborn child that he had to leave my home. Regardless of his response, I needed to be stern in my decision.

Later that evening he came to the house and I shared with him my experience at church. I told him that I accepted Jesus as my Savior and Lord, and that I could no longer live like before. Up until now, I hadn't shared with you that he was a Muslim man who knew I had been raised Christian. According to him, in Islamic belief they are free to involve themselves with someone of another faith. When we first met, it wasn't a big deal to me because I wasn't following anything but myself. I went on explaining that he had to leave my home once and for all because I needed to focus on seeking God to fix my life. He hit the roof, wanted to argue about my decision. He didn't see how wanting to serve God had anything to do with him living with me, especially when I was about to have his child. At this point, I was not about to argue and give an explanation or justify my made-up mind. It was not up for discussion.

He got up to leave in a rage. I asked for my house's keys, which just escalated his unruly behavior. He said, "No" and proceeded to leave. I knew things would spiral out of control with his temperament and mine so I didn't ask again or be combative. I didn't get my keys back. He didn't move out but I kept my distance and continued my search to know God. I continued going to church. What's so ironic is that he would stay away from the house for days and would always show up on Sunday morning while I waited for my ride to church. He would be intoxicated in my face, telling me I wasn't going to church. Of course, we bickered back and forth until the horn blew for me to come out side.

Finally, I went into labor and gave birth to a beautiful baby boy whom I named Paul. The first few weeks were really tough for me since I had to deal with his obscene behavior, his continued intoxication, and care for three children. When he would come to the house intoxicated, he would always want to take our son outside with him. I would tell him I didn't think it was a good idea because he had been breastfed. Furthermore, he had no way of feeding him. Of course, that meant nothing to him. At one point, I got so fed up that I called the police. When they showed up to my door, I was informed that if I didn't have custody papers there was nothing they could do. He had the same rights as me. It didn't matter to them that I stressed he was acting inappropriately.

29

Misery: the Path for Liberty

"[O Lord] remember [earnestly] my affliction and my misery, my wandering and my outcast state, the wormwood and the gall." (Lamentations 3:19)

All I could do was to pray and keep asking God to deliver me from the strife and heartache of my life. I no longer wanted my children to watch me go through such turmoil, seeming helpless yet telling them that God was going to change our lives. I set some rules in my home. I made it known that I did not want unclean things in my house. That meant no drinking, gambling, or loud music filled with cursing. He agreed to respect my decision but continued to make broken promises not to do these things.

I remember this incident like it was yesterday. I was attempting to use the bathroom but he was in there. I waited for him to come out so I can go in. I knew he had been drinking. But I wasn't sure when he was drinking because it was rather early in the day and he had only been out once so far. When I went to use the bathroom, I discovered a half-empty, forty-ounce beer bottle behind the toilet. That was it for me! I stormed out of the bathroom into the bedroom, where he was, and told him to get out. He jumped up in my face, stating he wasn't going anywhere. I told him if he didn't leave on his own this time, I would have the law remove him. He pushed me and I pushed him back. He then mugged me in the face and his fingernails cut me near my eye. I started to fight then and he pushed me on the floor. Then he ran out of the bedroom, proceeding down the stairs. I jumped up, grabbed the iron off the wardrobe, and tried to hit him over the banister. As he fled, the iron just missed his head. Out the front door he went.

The baby and I were the only two at home. My other children were in school. I sat on the couch and cried my eyes and heart out, pleading with God to save me before I die or do something to destroy my life forever. The load was too much that I could no longer bare it.

Low and behold, about thirty minutes later there was a knock at the door as if someone wanted to break it down. I thought it was he, so I looked out the window first. To my surprise, it was two detectives. I went downstairs and opened the door. A woman and a man stood there. They identified themselves and explained that the nature of their visit was by way of a warrant for the arrest of my child's father. I told them he was not there and they told me that they had to search the house. I allowed them to come in. The woman asked if I was okay, because it was apparent that I had been in a fight. I told her, "No" but that I would be fine.

After the gentleman searched the house, discovering he was not there, he turned to me and asked for my name. Then he said, "Ma'am I'm sorry to inform you we have a warrant for your arrest as well." He asked if there was anyone who could get the baby. I said, "No" and his reply was, "We will have to take him down and have child custody services pick him up." He then explained that the arrest was for "murder in the first degree" amongst other charges.

My heart hit the floor but this seemed like the best day of my life. I knew that I hadn't killed anyone. But if being free from my misery meant going to prison I was ready. There was a peace overshadowing me that I had never felt before this day. The detectives were kind and did not put cuffs on me. They placed my baby on my lap for the ride down. They also explained that they would give me a chance to call someone to pick him up before they notify child custody services. God was with me all along. I asked and believed Him to save me. However, I didn't know how He was going to do so.

I was able to reach my father at home. I explained to him my whereabouts and why I was there. He couldn't believe what he was hearing and told me that he was on his way. Once my father arrived at the police station, I was unable to speak with him. The detectives explained why they arrested me and what he needed to do. An officer came to communicate that they couldn't release my son to my father because he was too upset, screaming and shouting that they had no right to arrest me. So it would be an endangerment to allow my father to take my son.

I was grateful they allowed me another call. This time I was forced to call my mother at work. It is something I dreaded doing because I knew my mother wouldn't be able to handle this well. I called her and shared some details. I asked her to come pick up my son. While I waited patiently for my mother to show up, God was speaking to me. He assured me that I didn't have to fear because He was with me and would set me free by way of truth. I could feel God's love, peace, and protection.

My mother finally arrived and was given the details by the detectives. They then allowed her to come where I was to get my son and speak with me. My mother began to cry. She didn't fully understand what was going on because of the charges against me. She hugged me so tightly around my neck. I could feel her pain but a part of me was cold and empty wanting to blame my dad and her for where I ended up.

The detectives told her that she had to leave but she wouldn't let go of my neck. Finally, I told her I was okay and God was going to set me free. She asked me not to say anything and that they would hire me a lawyer. What my parents didn't understand was that the charges brought against me had no power to keep me in prison because they were a lie. This was God's way of leading me to the path of liberty and healing. A road I had never taken my entire life.

Once my mother left, the detectives begin to question me. All I could hear was God speaking to me, "The truth will set you free," a verse I heard numerous times when I was growing up. At this point, I understood what God expected of me and how I would be released from the life of misery I had been living. Finally, I gave my statement and thought I was going to be let go.

30

The Road to Prison

"For the Lord hears the poor and needy and despises not His prisoners (His miserable and wounded ones)." (Psalm 69:33)

However, that was the start of my heels turning down into an unexpected road to prison. I was processed, booked, and taken to a holding cell where I waited with other inmates to see a judge. I was now feeling confused because I didn't quite know what God was doing. My thoughts were after doing what was right. I would be released to go home not knowing that God didn't just want me to return home, He wanted to transform my life forevermore.

As I sat in the crowded cell with other women, who had been arrested for various reasons, I had to keep my cool and be strong. Women were crying upon their return from seeing the judge. They were afraid they wouldn't be able to go home because of the bails that were being set. My mind was racing and wondering what would happen in my case, because my charges were more serious than the other women's.

In the early morning hours, approximatively two o'clock, I was called to see a judge via satellite on a television screen. I could see the courtroom filled with family and friends who could see me on the screen as well. People were crying and their countenance was sad, which made me feel sorry. I can remember saying to myself, "Where were all of you when I was ready to kill myself? Where were all of you when I was being abused and mistreated? And why are you all here when I was just a rebellious child who never listened and wouldn't amount to anything?" I was angry and bitter towards them all. I didn't feel as though they were genuinely concerned about my wellbeing but instead wanted to see what happened to me.

The judge listened to the charges against me, and the district attorney requested that I be held in prison without bail because the charges were capitol. The judge argued that they had no evidence and pointed that I had never been in trouble with the law before now. The district attorney continued to argue his case. The judge ruled in his favor. So I was taken back to my cell, disturbed and not knowing what to expect at this point.

The guards explained that my family would now have to appeal the decision, and if granted I would go before another judge. I waited and waited, praying to God for help. Suddenly I began to recount with God the miracles He had done that I read about in the Bible and believed including opening blind eyes, healing the sick, and feeding multitudes with five loaves of bread and two fish. I told God if He could do all those miraculous things then I knew He could get me out of prison.

Finally, my name was called to see another judge. The hearing was similar to the other one, except this time the judge didn't agree with what the district attorney wanted to do. He granted me a hundred thousand dollar bail, of which my family would have to pay ten thousands for me to be released. That was not enough for the district attorney. He asked if one of the conditions could be twenty-four hour house arrest so I wouldn't flee. The judge explained that he didn't think I was a flight risk but made it of the stipulations in order for me to be released from prison.

After the hearing was over, I was taken back to my holding cell. Because I had never been in prison before, I was unfamiliar with the process after given a sentence. I thought the guards were going to come and let me out once my bail was paid. I asked the female guard what would happen next. She stated that I would be transferred to the county prison to wait for my bail to be paid. That crushed me because I thought to myself that I can't go to a bigger prison with more women. I knew my temperament would cause me to fight if someone bothered me.

As I waited to be transferred, I prayed and asked God to protect and keep me. I was afraid of getting into more trouble and not going home. Finally, it was time to be transferred with other women. We were all shackled and transported to the county prison for women. Upon arrival I was frisked, given a prison uniform, processed, and placed in what they call "quarantine" for twenty-four hours. I was with no interactions before I was assigned to be with other inmates based upon my charges. The cell I was placed in was very small with a tiny window. I could look out and see the road. This was my breaking point. I began looking out the window, watching cars race down the highway and thinking to myself if I could just make it to the road I could go home and hug my children. I wanted to touch my children so badly but couldn't.

God began to speak to me. He reminded me of all the times I chose men, partying, and running the streets over being with my children. He told me that the pain I was feeling was the same pain my children felt every time I neglected them. All I could do was to cry and express to God how sorry I was. I asked Him to heal my children of such pain and help them forgive me someday. God assured me that my life would never be the same after I was released from prison. He had a plan for my life and if I trust and obey Him he would bring it to past. He told me that He understood my choices. He knew all about the pain I suffered throughout my life. He knew I was broken but He was a mender and would put my life back together again. He promised me that I was getting a second chance at the life He originally planned for me. He told me that I was there because He had chosen me before I was born, and He had a purpose for my entire life.

I cried myself to sleep. Before I knew it, the sun rose and it was morning. I paced the floor all morning, praying to God and expressing all my hurt, uncertainties, insecurities, and worries. I asked God questions about how He was going to get me out but He gave no response. I heard my name called on the intercom and a guard came to my cell. She explained that my bail had been posted. As soon as I was about to thank God, she said but that I can't be released from prison until the house arrest division comes to pick me up and take me home so I could be monitored around the clock. I asked when that would be and she said that it could take days, weeks, or months. At this point, I wanted to die. I felt like God had deserted me. She said that I would now come out of the quarantine and be taken to a block with other murderers, and with those who attempted to murder. My heart dropped and all I kept was that either I'm going to get hurt or I'm going to hurt someone.

As I was being transferred to what they call "D block" a song kept ringing in my spirit "Jesus be a fence all around me every day. Jesus, I need you to protect me as I travel along the way. I know you can, yes, Lord, I know you will, yes, Lord. Fight my battles, yes, Lord, if I keep still, yes, Lord. Lord, be a fence all around me every day."

We arrived to my cell and I was introduced to my cellmate. Thank God, she was an older woman who didn't appear to want any trouble. She and I conversed for a while, sharing why we were incarcerated and the like. She assured me that I would be okay just by staying to myself. For the first few days, I had no idea what to do with myself. Everything was routine, so I spent most of my time in my cell not wanting to associate with any one. I came out for meals, showers, and yard time. I knew that I didn't belong there. I was different than most of the women I had seen. I was given phone privileges to call my family, which would only make me sadder especially speaking with my mother and hearing the voice of my children.

31

Forgiveness: The Road to Healing

"For if you forgive people their trespasses [their reckless and willful sins, leaving them, letting them go, and giving up resentment], your heavenly Father will also forgive you." (Matthew 6:14)

I met a woman by the name of Rita who had been there for some time and was highly involved in the church services. She asked me to accompany her and I did. This was more than what I anticipated. She helped sustain me while I was there. The services were like none of the ones I had experienced on the outside world. Women would come together and worship God, cry together, and receive love and affection from the ministers that were there.

I made it a part of my day to attend the services. I was being healed, growing closer to God. I was given a

Bible. For the first time, I started to read all about who God is from beginning to end. I no longer asked God to release me from prison; rather I started to pray for a new heart and mind. God would visit me in my cell, wake me out of my sleep, and speak His word to me. I remember praying one night and suddenly I began speaking in the tongues of the Holy Spirit, which was something I hadn't done before and God told me what I was saying. I grew closer to God. For the first time after being imprisoned for two weeks, I came to the conclusion that even if I never got released, I had been made free and would survive.

As I continued going to services and being ministered to, I was made aware that I had to forgive everyone that hurt me or that I felt ill about as God would forgive me and give me a new life. I was told that I had to let go of my past and all that was done to me if I wanted my life to change. I didn't quite know how to do such things but in prayer I asked God to help me because I wanted a new life in Him. God told me that people don't always intend to hurt us. They have no way of knowing when they hurt us because to them they're doing what they think is best based on what they know. So I needed to forgive them and show them a better way as I learn.

When God opened up my understanding and gave me a different perspective on the things people do I was able to feel compassion towards them instead of bitterness and resentment. I figured they didn't know any better and I was chosen by God to be an example of something different. I first asked God to forgive me for holding grudges, hatred in my heart towards people who handled me ignorantly, and to remove the feelings of pain and emptiness from them. I declared that I forgave any and every one known and unknown whom I felt hurt me in any manner. I let them go and opened my heart to receiving them. Instantly, I could feel a weight lifted from me. I was ready to take another road to receive the healing that I needed.

One week later the house arrest division came to get me out of prison. All I remember was that my name was called over the intercom to grab all my belongings. My cellmate said, "You're going home. It's your time. Remember what God did for you and never look back." Tears rolled down my face as we hugged and said our farewells. She helped me gather my belongings and proceeded to the guard station. I asked if I could tell Rita goodbye first and they granted me that request. Rita was astound rejoicing with me. She told me that I was chosen by God to make a difference in the world and that she would be looking forward to hearing about me later in life. I hugged her as tight as I could and told her, "Thank you for everything, especially believing in me and leading me to God."

32

From Brokenness to Leadership

"The Lord is close to those who are of a broken heart and saves such as are crushed with sorrow for sin and are humbly and thoroughly penitent." (Psalm 34:18)

A s I left the prison with the officers, I was nervous not knowing what to expect when I get home. I was unsure how others would receive the new me. I was also uncertain if I had the strength to face all I left behind.

On the ride home, I asked God for the reasons He took me through all this, besides the experience I had with Him. He told me that, before I was conceived, He chose me to be His deliverer, to bring Him glory, and to lead others to Him. He placed His hand upon my life. Despite all I've had to endure and suffer, He knew that I would make it through. He anointed me and equipped me for the journey I had to take. He made me a leader from childhood that many would follow my example. The life I lived in the streets influenced and empowered others. Yet I was blinded by darkness and could not see the impact I had on lives. I was the ringleader to many who professed God but joined me in sin. So God chose to break me in a manner He knew only me could walk through. He prepared me throughout my entire life for what I am going through now. God was certain if He took me down and raise me back up, the rest would no longer play church. Just like any other time, they would follow my leading and seek personal relationships with God as well.

I must have cried the entire ride home as God was speaking to me. It was in those moments that I realized that my life had purpose and power to change the lives of others. All I had to do from that point on was to follow God's lead no matter what.

God assured me, before arriving to the house, that I would be as His servant Moses and set His people free. He promised me that I would be as His prophet Jeremiah, rooting out, pulling down, destroying, overthrowing, building, and planting. Finally yet importantly, God showed me that I would make disciples and teach people to have a personal relationship with Him. I had no idea how God was going to do all that through the little old me, but I took His word to heart and believed what He promised me, knowing that one day I would see it come to fruition. At that particular time, all I knew is that I loved God and wanted to spend the rest of my life serving Him. I was forever grateful for what He had done in my life and I desired for everyone to experience Him as I did.

33

A Missionary...in the Kitchen!

"How beautiful upon the mountains are the feet of him who brings good tidings, who publishes peace, who brings good tidings of good, who publishes salvation." (Isaiah 52:7)

A t the front door my, dad opened the door with a big smile and hugged me tight. I thought to myself, "Wow, what I have been through has really changed you" because that's not a reaction I was used to get from him. As I entered the house, it was flooded with family, friends, church members, and most of all my children. All were waiting and anticipating welcoming me home. It was a little awkward because everyone was starring and waiting for a reaction. They were all so familiar with me showing up as the life of the party. But this time I was meek, gentle, and calm. It was a "me" they have never seen, and a side of me I had never known myself. To break the ice, I started to give out hugs and thank everyone for their love and support. My mother stood there waiting for her hug patiently as everyone else bombarded me. Oh boy, when it was her turn she didn't want to let go of me, same as my children and siblings.

My mother had cooked a big dinner for everyone. This is something she loved doing. She knew I hadn't tasted a good, home-cooked meal in three weeks. As we were eating, I sat quietly, watching everyone laughing and fellowshipping with one another. I could discern that some wanted to hear about my experience behind bars but were too afraid to ask. As time went on, people were scattered all over the house. My cousins, sisters, mom, and I remained in the kitchen. Someone stated that I was different and very quiet. It was something no one was used too.

Finally, the mystery question was asked, "How was it in prison? How did you make it in there that long?" I was relieved that one person conjured up enough gut to ask me, instead of letting everyone keep curious. Now it was time for me to share what God had allowed to happen to me and the reason for it.

I began by sharing all that I had been through up until my arrest. Then I told them about how God all the while was trying to reconcile me back to Himself and how

136

the circumstances were the only way it could happen. I apologized for destructively leading my life and setting a bad example before my encounter with God. I explained that God wanted each and every one of us to give Him our heart and soul. We must no longer play church or live contrary to His word and what was required of believers.

I told them that God made an example out of me. That is because I was the ringleader, the fighter, the one bold enough to take risk, the one who didn't care how others have seen me, the one who didn't hide behind church but was out in the open with everything, and the go-to person for anything. God was certain that if He changed my life, those of the world who followed me would in fact follow me in Him.

Before I knew it, as I was speaking people was crying, shouting, jumping, and falling on the kitchen floor. I wasn't sure what was happening. All I knew is that I was speaking what God laid on my heart to share with my family and friends. I began to cry, as I continued to speak, pleading with everyone to get right with God because He loved us so much and had big plans for our lives. I pleaded that we no longer should play with God but get serious about our relationship with Him. We should no more go to church on Sunday and live worldly the rest of the week. I had the attention of all those who gathered even those who were walking. God touched the straight and narrow as He used me in that kitchen. That was my very first platform to declare the glory of God and His power fell upon us.

What I experienced in prison with God one-on-one He allowed others to share in this same experience that day. Our lives were never the same. We all started to live holy and seek after God. We stopped all the partying, living worldly, and serving God only from our lips. Instead, we began to serve Him from our hearts.

It was great to be back home with my family, from whom I had wondered away my entire life thus far. I had no understanding that my parents knew there was something special about me and were trying to protect me from the life of destruction I ended up living. Yet out of ignorance, they went about it the wrong way. My mother told me that, when I was five years old, God spoke to her about me saying that He called me to preach His word and declare His glory in the earth. She stated that while I was gone from home so many years, all that she had to hold on to was the word she received from the Lord.

I remained on house arrest until my court date.

That's where God showed Himself strong on my behalf. Not only was I released from house arrest, the record was completely erased as if I was never in trouble with the law, having a clean slate. The ten thousand dollar bail was also returned in full. I failed to mention prior that God touched my favorite uncle Beanie's heart to pay the bail for me to be released from prison. God worked things out in my favor. Although I had a home of my own, I didn't want to return there where there were too many bad memories. Because of where I had been, I desired to move forward, never looking back unless I was helping someone else move forward. I continued on my personal journey with God to better understand some of the things I had been through. Things like the relationships with men and why they didn't last.

PART 5

THE JOURNEY'S LEAD TO

WHOLENESS

34

From Ugly Caterpillar to Beautiful Butterfly

"For the Lord takes pleasure in His people; He will beautify the humble with salvation and adorn the wretched with victory." (Psalm 149:4)

I discovered that there were major needs unmet in my life, like affection, communication, acceptance, support, proper guidance, and nurturing. I had also been physically and psychologically abused, and emotionally neglected. These were voids in my life that I desired to fill. I once tried to do so in relationships with men, who themselves had some of the same voids and were empty just as I was. I was immature and only knew love to a degree, which was not deep enough to remove my emptiness.

My heart and soul were shattered into pieces because I would give so much of myself in relationships and friendships yet didn't receive the same in return. This would always leave stripped from one to the other. I trusted the most valuable parts of me to people who were not equipped nor trustworthy to care for them. What I longed for was supposed to be given me as a child. It was not until I realized that what I needed, at this point in my life, could only come from God first. Then I could have healthy relationships where I experience it from others.

With each passing day, I grew closer to God, receiving a love that's unexplainable. He won my affections. He listened when I talked and spoke back to me. He told me that I was once an ugly caterpillar but was now His beautiful butterfly. He told me that I was as a diamond, ruby, a pure gold, and a queen. Of course, I wasn't sure what all that meant but I researched and studied each description that He gave me of myself. He gave me a clear understanding of what He meant.

I began growing rapidly in my walk with God. I had one desire and that was to please Him. As I matured, God began to use me in ministry. People would prophesy things to me that I never imagined to be so. Many couldn't believe the transformation, and many more didn't want to receive it.

One day while sitting in Sunday school, my childhood sweetheart came in and sat behind me. I hadn't seen him regularly in eleven years. We met in the same church came back during VBS. At about twelve and fourteen years of age we called ourselves, liking one another. His mother was married to my uncle by marriage. We got to see a lot of one another because we would meet at Simon's playground when I stayed at my aunt's house. None of the adults knew we were sweethearts. They looked at us as cousins. His mother ended up leaving the church to attend another. So we were separated and that broke my little heart at the time. Neither of us knew that God had chosen us to spend eternity together. When He sat behind me in church it was like I could feel him. I turned around and there he was. We said hello and I turned back around quickly. My youngest child was about nine months.

As good as it was to see him, I really was focusing on serving God. We interacted and saw one another in the church service that he faithfully attended as well as I did. Eventually, we exchanged phone numbers and began to communicate outside of church. Here it is fourteen years later and we are happily married and serving God together.

APOSTLE FREE HILL

35

The Journey's Pain Produced a Promise

"For I consider that the sufferings of this present time (this present life) are not worth being compared with the glory that is about to be revealed to us and in us and for us and conferred on us!" (Romans 8:18)

S ome may say your journey was all over the place. Yes, my life was wandering from here to there and everywhere, until I met Jesus who put my wandering to an end. He showed me what was wrong, how to make it right, and promised me a beautiful future if I followed His leading. No, I couldn't undo what was done but I could start over and control how things turn out. The truth is that my parents couldn't have raised me different. My relationships with men could've turned out better. All the pain that I had to feel was all part of the journey to freedom and wholeness.

If I hadn't been rejected, I would have never learned

how to accept people the way they come and never leave them the way they are. If I wasn't misunderstood, I wouldn't have a strong passion to seek understanding before coming to a conclusion regarding a person or a matter. If my heart was never broken, or my emotions torn to pieces, I wouldn't know God's power to mend and heal those that are broken. If I was never looked upon as a "stupid nobody," I would have never returned to school to obtain my high school diploma and college credits towards my bachelor's degree in Psychology. If I never lacked genuine love, I would have never sought after God who is love and never have to mistake it for nothing or no one again.

God took all my pain and produced promise. He chose me to be a deliverer to lead His people to freedom. That's why I had to know what it was like to be bound. This is why at a young age God had to separate me from my family members who were in religious bondage. It is all that one day I could return and set them free. I had to be broken to receive the power to heal and make whole again. I was once *lost in the wilderness of life* but now I am *found in the heart of God*, serving His kingdom and impacting the lives of others. Now I am a ringleader for God, a warrior against all darkness, filled with God's love and compassion, and available to others in need. I was not afraid to face my past, take responsibility for my own choices, and give my heart to the God who could heal and make it whole again. God gave me His character and attributes.

APOSTLE FREE HILL

36

Obedience is Better Than Sacrifice

"Behold, to obey is better than sacrifice, and to hearken than the fat of rams." (1 Samuel 15:22)

In 2004, God moved my family and me to North Carolina where He exalted me. I was ordained as a Minster of the Gospel of Jesus Christ; something I was diligently doing in my hometown but people couldn't get past who I was. I had grown beautifully in God, invested in who I was by taking courses, being imparted in, and having my gifts activated so I could effectively serve in Ministry. However, people kept trying to hold me back. When God told us to go, we obeyed and He tremendously blessed us. He sent us to a foreign land where no one knew us. But they recognized who we were when we arrived. God's hand was upon our lives. He used us in the lives of His people.

When our assignment was over, He sent us back to Philadelphia, PA. I cried and asked God if we fail Him. His answer was, "No daughter, you must return because my people you left behind are in Egypt religious bondage. I need you to go set them free." I went back and forth with God, asking if there were another way. But His answer was the same, to return home for His glory. He promised that He would prosper the work of my hands and my labor of love would not be in vain. We obeyed, of course, but our leaving broke the hearts of all we left behind. However, as God's Word instructs us that, "to obey is better than sacrifice" (1 Samuel 15:22).

I was under the impression that God wanted me to set the church members free. To my surprise, He called me to free the leaders. The prayer, warring, and labor were great but I did what God sent me back to my hometown to do. It took seven years before I have seen results but God accomplished what He promised.

After seven years of laboring, I was affirmed at the Philadelphia Convention Center as an Apostle, not by the leadership with whom I was laboring. God used me to raise up leaders and people, all for His name's sake. He exalted me while laboring. At this time in my life, God has been speaking more to me about ministering to leaders. He told me that I was like Paul the Apostle but I haven't thought much of it. God continues to deal with me about who I am. He told me to make my call and election sure (see 2 Peter 1:10).

About a year before the affirmation, God was encouraging me to study what an Apostle is and He showed me that I had already been doing the work. I studied the character, personality, temperament, purpose, passion, and work of an Apostle. It all described me in detail. I accepted the heavenly call and election of God upon my life. He allowed people to acknowledge it here on the earth. I never sought God for things or titles. I always sought to have His heart, think like Him, and have His appetite and passion. He gave it all to me.

God equipped, trained, tried, and proved me. Then He brought me forth as a pure gold. Today I can say that I know God in the fellowship of His suffering and I know Him in the power of His resurrection (see Philippians 3:10). I know that I have been chosen by God to be a prophetic intercessor and prayer warrior, to set His people free, to minister His healing, and reconcile people back to Him.

The journey to my purpose was painful, yet now it

is promising. I win every time and am certain to reach my destiny. I have gone through the wilderness and fought many giants along the way. Now I'm entering into my promise land and living life more abundantly. I understand with clarity the journey I had to take and the process I had to go through. I know that my salvation was free because Jesus paid the price, but my yoke-destroying anointing cost me everything. Freedom and wholeness is the outcome of the journey. Like Martin Luther King Jr., I shout from the mountaintop "Let Freedom Ring." Behold the glory of Jesus Christ my King.

WHEN YOUR HEELS NEED TO BE HEALED

PART 6

SCRIPTURES FOR FREEDOM

AND HEALING

37

For Freedom Christ Has Set Us Free

"In [this] freedom Christ has made us free [and completely liberated us]; stand fast then, and do not be hampered and held ensnared and submit again to a yoke of slavery [which you have once put off]." (Galatians 5:1)

Many of us will set out on the journey that takes us to the best of ourselves. Yet for many of us, the journey is short lived, mainly because of the bumps and bruises that come along the journey. We discover in the course of our journey that life does not always bow down to our expectations, no matter who we are. No person is immune to conflict, whether it's a hardship, unfulfilled expectations, rejection, or just facing the day-to-day issues in dealing in life. Unfortunately, many of us crumble under the pressure and become hopeless. With great sense of unfairness and defeat, we allow ourselves to be tossed back and forth by the waves of life and soon settle down for a life not our own.

The Word of God, the Bible, opens our eyes to the freedom and wholeness that we can experience in Christ. It is because of Christ's complete work of atonement on the cross for us, that we can enjoy freedom over sin and darkness of this world if we trust in Him. Therefore, below are some biblical verses, listed chronologically as they appear in the books of the Bible, that I pray as you read and meditate on them they will encourage you in your journey to healing from any brokenness you might have.

Leviticus 25:10 "And you shall hallow the fiftieth year and proclaim liberty throughout all the land to all its inhabitants. It shall be a jubilee for you; and each of you shall return to his ancestral possession [which through poverty he was compelled to sell], and each of you shall return to his family [from whom he was separated in bond service]."

Psalm 30:2–3 "O Lord my God, I cried to You and You have healed me. O Lord, You have brought my life up from Sheol (the place of the dead); You have kept me alive, that I should not go down to the pit (the grave)."

Psalm 147:3 "He heals the brokenhearted and binds up their wounds [curing their pains and their sorrows]."

Proverbs 17:22 "A happy heart is good medicine *and* a

cheerful mind works healing, but a broken spirit dries up the bones."

Isaiah 40:31 "But those who wait for the Lord [who expect, look for, and hope in Him] shall change *and* renew their strength *and* power; they shall lift their wings *and* mount up [close to God] as eagles [mount up to the sun]; they shall run and not be weary, they shall walk and not faint *or* become tired."

Isaiah 53:5 "But He was wounded for our transgressions, He was bruised for our guilt *and* iniquities; the chastisement [needful to obtain] peace *and* well-being for us was upon Him, and with the stripes [that wounded] Him we are healed *and* made whole."

Isaiah 58:6–7 "[Rather] is not this the fast that I have chosen: to loose the bonds of wickedness, to undo the bands of the yoke, to let the oppressed go free, and that you break every [enslaving] yoke? Is it not to divide your bread with the hungry and bring the homeless poor into your house—when you see the naked, that you cover him, and that you hide not yourself from [the needs of] your own flesh *and* blood?"

Isaiah 61:1–3 "The Spirit of the Lord God is upon me, because the Lord has anointed *and* qualified me to preach the Gospel *of* good tidings to the meek, the poor, *and* afflicted; He has sent me to bind up *and* heal the brokenhearted, to proclaim liberty to the [physical and spiritual] captives and the opening of the prison *and* of the eyes to those who are bound, To proclaim the acceptable year of the Lord [the year of His favor] and the day of vengeance of our God, to comfort all who mourn, To grant [consolation and joy] to those who mourn in Zion—to give them an ornament (a garland or diadem) of beauty instead of ashes, the oil of joy instead of mourning, the garment [expressive] of praise instead of a heavy, burdened, *and* failing spirit—that they may be called oaks of righteousness [lofty, strong, and magnificent, distinguished for uprightness, justice, and right standing with God], the planting of the Lord, that He may be glorified."

Jeremiah 30:17 "For I will restore health to you, and I will heal your wounds, says the Lord, because they have called you an outcast, saying, This is Zion, whom no one seeks after *and* for whom no one cares!"

Mark 10:52 "And Jesus said to him, Go your way; your faith has healed you. And at once he received his sight and accompanied Jesus on the road."

Mark 11:24 "for this reason I am telling you, whatever you ask for in prayer, believe (trust and be confident) that it is granted to you, and you will [get it]."

John 3:16–17 "For God so greatly loved *and* dearly prized the world that He [even] gave up His only begotten (unique) Son, so that whoever believes in (trusts in, clings to, relies on) Him shall not perish (come to destruction, be lost) but have eternal (everlasting) life. For God did not send the Son into the world in order to judge (to reject, to condemn, to pass sentence on) the world, but that the world might find salvation *and* be made safe *and* sound through Him."

John 8:32 "And you will know the Truth, and the Truth will set you free."

John 8:36 "So if the Son liberates you [makes you free men], then you are really *and* unquestionably free."

John 10:10 "The thief comes only in order to steal and kill and destroy. I came that they may have *and* enjoy life, and have it in abundance (to the full, till it overflows)."

Acts 4:11–12 "This [Jesus] is the Stone which was despised *and* rejected by you, the builders, but which has become the Head of the corner [the Cornerstone]. And there is salvation in *and* through no one else, for there is no other name under heaven given among men by *and* in which we must be saved."

Acts 13:39 "And that through Him everyone who believes [who acknowledges Jesus as his Savior and devotes himself to Him] is absolved (cleared and freed) from every charge from which he could not be justified *and* freed by the Law of Moses *and* given right standing with God."

Romans 6:7 "For when a man dies, he is freed (loosed, delivered) from [the power of] sin [among men]."

Romans 6:18 "And having been set free from sin, you have become the servants of righteousness (of conformity to the divine will in thought, purpose, and action)."

Romans 6:22 "But now since you have been set free from sin and have become the slaves of God, you have your present reward in holiness and its end is eternal life."

Romans 8:1–4 "Therefore, [there is] now no condemnation (no adjudging guilty of wrong) for those who are in Christ Jesus, *who live [and] walk not after the dictates of the flesh, but after the dictates of the Spirit.* For the law of the Spirit of life [which is] in Christ Jesus [the law of our new being] has freed me from the law of sin and of death. For God has done what the Law could not do, [its power] being weakened by the flesh [the entire nature of man without the Holy Spirit]. Sending His own Son in the guise of sinful flesh and as an offering for sin, [God] condemned sin in the flesh [subdued, overcame, deprived it of its power over all who accept that sacrifice], So that the righteous *and* just requirement of the Law might be fully met in us who live *and* move not in the ways of the flesh but in the ways of the Spirit [our lives governed not by the standards and according to the dictates of the flesh, but controlled by the Holy Spirit]."

Romans 8:21 "That nature (creation) itself will be set free from its bondage to decay *and* corruption [and gain an entrance] into the glorious freedom of God's children."

Romans 10:9–10 "Because if you acknowledge *and* confess with your lips that Jesus is Lord and in your heart believe (adhere to, trust in, and rely on the truth) that God raised Him from the dead, you will be saved. For with the heart a person believes (adheres to, trusts in, and relies on Christ) and so is justified (declared righteous, acceptable to

God), and with the mouth he confesses (declares openly and speaks out freely his faith) *and* confirms [his] salvation."

1 Corinthians 6:12 "Everything is permissible (allowable and lawful) for me; but not all things are helpful (good for me to do, expedient and profitable when considered with other things). Everything is lawful for me, but I will not become the slave of anything *or* be brought under its power."

1 Corinthians 9:19-20 "For although I am free in every way from anyone's control, I have made myself a bond servant to everyone, so that I might gain the more [for Christ]. To the Jews I became as a Jew, that I might win Jews; to men under the Law, [I became] as one under the Law, though not myself being under the Law, that I might win those under the Law."

2 Corinthians 3:17 "Now the Lord is the Spirit, and where the Spirit of the Lord is, there is liberty (emancipation from bondage, freedom)."

Galatians 5:1 "In [this] freedom Christ has made us free [and completely liberated us]; stand fast then, and do not be hampered *and* held ensnared *and* submit again to a yoke of slavery [which you have once put off]."

Galatians 5:13 "For you, brethren, were [indeed] called to freedom; only [do not let your] freedom be an incentive to your flesh *and* an opportunity *or* excuse [for selfishness], but through love you should serve one another."

Ephesians 6:17 "And take the helmet of salvation and the sword that the Spirit wields, which is the Word of God."

Philippians 2:14–15 "Do all things without grumbling *and* faultfinding *and* complaining [against God] and questioning *and* doubting [among yourselves], That you may show yourselves to be blameless *and* guileless, innocent *and* uncontaminated, children of God without blemish (faultless, unrebukable) in the midst of a crooked *and* wicked generation [spiritually perverted and perverse], among whom you are seen as bright lights (stars or beacons shining out clearly) in the [dark] world."

1 Thessalonians 5:17 "Be unceasing in prayer [praying perseveringly]."

2 Timothy 1:7 "For God did not give us a spirit of timidity (of cowardice, of craven and cringing and fawning fear), but [He has given us a spirit] of power and of love and of calm *and* well-balanced mind *and* discipline *and* self-control."

Hebrews 2:14–15 "Since, therefore, [these His] children share in flesh and blood [in the physical nature of human beings], He [Himself] in a similar manner partook of the same [nature], that by [going through] death He might bring to nought *and* make of no effect him who had the power of death—that is, the devil—And also that He might deliver *and* completely set free all those who through the [haunting] fear of death were held in bondage throughout the whole course of their lives."

James 1:25 "But he who looks carefully into the faultless law, the [law] of liberty, and is faithful to it *and* perseveres in looking into it, being not a heedless listener who forgets but an active doer [who obeys], he shall be blessed in his doing (his life of obedience)."

James 2:15–16 "If a brother or sister is poorly clad and lacks food for each day, And one of you says to him, Goodbye! Keep [yourself] warm and well fed, without giving him the necessities for the body, what good does that do?" [Live] as free people, [yet] without employing your freedom as a pretext for wickedness; but [live at all times] as servants of God."

1 Peter 2:16 "[Live] as free people, [yet] without employing your freedom as a pretext for wickedness; but [live at all times] as servants of God."

PART 7

AFFIRMATION,

DECLARATION, AND

DECREE

38

Finishing the Journey Well

"[For my determined purpose is] that I may know Him [that I may progressively become more deeply and intimately acquainted with Him, perceiving and recognizing and understanding the wonders of His Person more strongly and more clearly], and that I may in that same way come to know the power outflowing from His resurrection [which it exerts over believers], and that I may so share His sufferings as to be continually transformed [in spirit into His likeness even] to His death, [in the hope]." (Philippians 3:10)

What does not mean to finish the journey well? How does it look like? Is it to end life with a long and comfortable retirement? Is it to finish while having lots of stuff? Is it ending life with a pain-free death?

As we have seen throughout the journey in this book, "finishing well" means following Christ at every stage of life and to the very end of it, being set free to do

His well so at the end we hear Him say, "Well done, good and faithful servant."

It is by God's grace that we finish the race well. As John Newton put it in his famous hymn, "Tis grace hath brought me safe thus far, and grace will lead me home." Since we are kept in the journey by God's grace, it is then very appropriate to pray, "Lord, give me the grace to finish well."

We finish well when we have a *Christ-centered life*, knowing that we are saved by Him. Christ is the source of our life and the center of our affections. To live a life of liberty and progress unto wholeness we must have a personal relationship with Christ and walk daily with Him. Christ is "the Leader *and* the Source of our faith" (Hebrews 12:2).

We also finish well when we have a *focused life* on Christ and on the task that He has given to us. Knowing the purpose of life with clarity and constancy, and understanding of the gifts Christ has given us are key to finishing well. The Apostle Paul had a focused life. He once said, "one thing I do [it is my one aspiration]" (Philippians 3:13). He did not say, "These 50 things I dabble in."

We finish well when we have *disciplined lives*. Again, the Apostle Paul gives us the picture of a runner in the race. He encourages us to run in such a way that we may win at the end. He said, "Now every athlete who goes into training conducts himself temperately *and* restricts himself in all things...I buffet my body [handle it roughly, discipline it by hardships] and subdue it, for fear that after proclaiming to others the Gospel *and* things pertaining to it, I myself should become unfit [not stand the test, be unapproved and rejected as a counterfeit]." (1 Corinthians 9:25–27). Similarly, the author to the Hebrews said, "Therefore then, since we are surrounded by so great a cloud of witnesses [who have borne testimony to the Truth], let us strip off *and* throw aside every encumbrance (unnecessary weight) and that sin which so readily (deftly and cleverly) clings to *and* entangles us, and let us run with patient endurance *and* steady *and* active persistence the appointed course of the race that is set before us" (Hebrews 12:1).

We must also have a *teachable spirit* by maintaining a humble soul when receiving midcourse corrections. Throughout the journey, we need to be lifelong learners as we learn from reading, watching, listening to others, and from life itself. Paul, at the very end of his life, was still learning as he says to Timothy, "[When] you come, bring…also the books" (2 Timothy 4:13).

Success in our journey depends upon *key relationships* of faithful people who pray for us, keep us accountable, shepherd us, and encourage us. We can't run this life's race alone. With that mind, let's define some key terms to have a clear understanding of them.

Dictionary.com

Affirmation–*a statement or proposition that is declared to be true.*

Declaration–*formal statement or announcement; proclamation.*

Decree–*to command, ordain, decide by decree; a formal authoritative order.*

Now we turn to the affirmation, declaration, and decree. Please read it carefully and make the decision yourself.

I am a new person created in the image and likeness of God. I am fearfully and wonderfully made. I am heir with God and fellow heir with Christ Jesus. I am the light of the world, the salt of the earth, and a city on a hill that cannot be hidden. I am a royal priesthood, a chosen race, and a peculiar ambassador for God. I am in Christ Jesus and all old things in my life are passed away, behold the new has come. I am a branch connected to the vine, which is God. I am not a product of my past or my pain, but I am a person of promise and purpose. In God, I live, move, and have my being. I am delivered from every form of captivity, and yoke of bondage, because of Christ. I have given all of my issues to Christ and I am made whole. I am strong and resolute in Christ. I am not ashamed of the gospel of Jesus Christ for it is the power of God unto

169

salvation. Jesus is my Savior and Lord. I live a

life that is pleasing unto Him. By the grace of

God, I am clothed with humility. I have the mind

of Christ. I seek first the kingdom of God and His

righteousness and all other things are added unto

me. I walk by faith and not by sight. I pray

without ceasing. I am led and guided by the Spirit

of God into all truth. The Son of God has made

me free and I will not be entangled in any yoke of

bondage again. I have life and I have it more

abundantly. Freely have I received of the Lord

and freely I give unto others. I am a faithful

tither and a cheerful giver. Wealth and riches are

in my house and the devourer is rebuked. I have

power over all the powers of the enemy. I use the

gifts that God has given me to build His church. I

do great exploits in Jesus's name. Miracles,

signs, and wonders follow me because I believe in

Christ. All things are possible to me because I

believe in God. I present my body as a living

sacrifice, holy, pleasing, and acceptable to God. I

renew my mind daily and my life is transformed

by the knowledge of Christ. I am filled with God's

Spirit and His love. I have His mind and His

character. The motive and intent of my heart is

pure. I do all things unto the glory of God. I

make disciples and I lead people to God. I live

according to God's holy Word. I am liberated and

healed from all pain, abuse, misuse, neglect, and

abandonment of my past. I am forgiven, I am

healed, I am whole, and I am free. In the name of

Jesus. Amen!

To contact Apostle Free Hill for book signings and speaking engagements please send all inquiries to

bfreemin@gmail.com

Made in the USA
Middletown, DE
13 July 2015